AUF WIEDERSEHEN LADS

Malcolm Robinson,
Barry Hindmarch,
Robert Nichols
With contributions from Ben Sandall

First Published in 2009 by Dickson Books

ISBN No: 978-0-9560846-1-3

Design & Layout: Paul Forrest
Project Editor: Malcolm Robinson

A catalogue record for this book is available from the British Library

Auf Wiedersehen – is German, meaning 'Goodbye', or 'when we see again'. It was used as a German football terrace chant in the mid 90's to intimidate the opposition.

Auf Wiedersehen Pet – is a British sit com about British workers based on a building site abroad, during hard recession hit times, set in the 1980s and 2002-04. It depicts the typical banter between various regions of Britain, particularly the North East and features the region's top football clubs in it down the years.

Auf Wiedersehen Lads – derives from a combination of the two, adopting the principles of saying goodbye, coupled with the cheeky banter surrounding football supporters, the Armed Forces and the North.

Dedications, Thanks
& Acknowledgements…

In what began as a photo book opportunist idea back in June 2008, to say we have come a long way to what you have in your hand would be a callous under-statement. False hope from publishers to changing ideas, leading into a three-club dissection of a historic season, finally welcoming Hull to the party.

Since the diary notes were first written, a great deal has altered the way I view life. The sheer frightening concept of not knowing what is around the corner has relaxed my stance towards football, with the notion that if good health prevails, then there is nothing we can not conquer, all in good time.

It is with this in mind, that I wish my Dad – James Robinson, the speediest recov-ery in the world, along with all the love in the world; I'll be waiting in The Grange, ready for a pint. And to my Mum – Carol Robinson, all my love and support and to my wife, Angela, all my love and undivided attention – you might be able to have a normal husband back now! And to my family and friends thanks for the support.

Thanks to Barry Hindmarch, Rob Nichols and Ben Sandall for writing what can only be described as overwhelmingly hard diary notes on their respective be-loved football clubs. Thanks to Martyn McFadden, Andy Fury, Steve Wraith, Si-mon Watson (for the quality cartoons), Jamie Turnbull for Operation Jersey Cow, Karl Eccles for the morale, the design lads for a tremendous job, Niall Quinn for being Niall Quinn, Alastair Brownlee, Paul Robinson and Tony Jeffries for their forewords and anyone else I may have forgotten, you know who you are!

Lest we forget the fallen troops out in the conflict zone of Afghanistan, their debt we will forever be in.

Dedicated to the memory of good friend Ben Chandler, North East legend Sir Bobby Robson and to the town of Wootton Bassett – a truly remarkable place indeed.

Malcolm Robinson, August 2009.

I'd like to thank my parents Brian & Maureen for always encouraging (and as a child funding) my involvement in football, whether it is playing, watching or writing about it.

A mention to my little brother Tony, who is a season ticket holder at Sunderland. I don't wish to give away the story, but I think he will particularly enjoy the ending!

Finally thanks to Sarah, who has always believed in me.

Barry Hindmarch, August 2009.

Dedicated to my Mam and Dad, brother and all my family and friends and everyone at Fly Me To The Moon 1988-2009 not out. I hope Boro fans will forgive me for reliving the agonies of relegation.

Robert Nichols, August 2009.

Foreword
By Tony Jeffries

I am delighted to have been invited to write a few words for the foreword of Auf Wiedersehen Lads. When not focussing upon my fights during the last few months, the run in to the football season has grabbed my attention with both arms.

I have experienced similar feelings to the Sunderland players themselves, when representing my hometown City in the ring at the Crowtree Leisure Centre in May 2009. The passion of the crowd is second to none in the North East and Wearside in particular. Boxing and football have always been traditional workingman's sports in the area and this remains true to this day.

This book is a reflection of commitment, loyalty and honesty – the latter renowned to the region's people, who say it like it is, no holds barred! It is a varied collection of thoughts, displaying the daily effort fans go to, not only in watching their team, but living life through their football club.

If the Olympiad events included a contest of sports fans, then surely the Gold medal would be finding its way to the North East of England.

Good luck and best wishes with the book lads.

Tony Jeffries
Olympic Bronze Medallist,
Boxing, Light Heavyweight Division.

Foreword
By Paul Robinson

It gives me great pride to be asked to write a few words for this book, having been fortunate enough to represent Sunderland Boys, Darlington and Newcastle United in my football career.

With that, I also found it hard to watch throughout the season, as all three clubs faced a battle for their status. Darlington, who went into administration battled for their existence, whilst Newcastle and Sunderland (along with Middlesbrough) traded blows to see who would survive in the top flight.

It was never in question that through the agonies of being a North East fan, there is not one second where football is not on the mind, doubly so this season, with never a dull moment in store in the region's favourite sport. This book reflects the passion, the stress, the banter and wit, not only associated with the game, but also of the area. I am sure, like me, you will be left thrilled, depressed, elated, squirming in your seat and much, much more, flicking through these pages.

It is without doubt a source of North East history, to be viewed over the months and years to come.

All the best,

Paul Robinson.
Sunderland Boys Pre-1994
Darlington Football Club 1994-1998
Newcastle United Football Club 1998-2000

Foreword
By Alastair Brownlee

As a Middlesbrough fan, covering every game for BBC Tees Sport and then talking about football every weeknight would normally come under the heading dream job, but, sadly, for much of season 2008-09 on the pitch the dream rapidly turned into a nightmare.

Supporters of Newcastle and Sunderland went through, I am sure, similar emotions although for fans at the Stadium of Light there was the not so small consolation of survival.

So why look back on a traumatic season?

Well, there is a hope that lessons have been learned and that better times lie ahead for all our teams and then there is also that fascination, even though you know the ending, of going back over months that left even die hard fans questioning their sanity at going through another 90 minutes of footballing torture!

You could, of course, live in the land of what might have beens, if only Downing had not been injured against Aston Villa, if only Mark Schwarzer had not kept a clean sheet on his Riverside return but I am sure all clubs have their own moments like that.

I prefer to hope that Boro, with a rich crop of young talent, can bounce back at the first time of asking and that the Riverside scoreboard will once again show Boro 2 Liverpool 0 in front of a capacity crowd!

That's football, even in the darkest times fans can always cling to the dream that tomorrow will be better... and the Premier League will be better once Boro, Newcastle and Sunderland are all back in the top flight.

Alastair Brownlee
BBC Tees Sport.

Introduction

STADIUM OF LIGHT

'All of a sudden, my heart is pounding non-stop. It's either the onset of a heart attack or the annual symptoms of Sunderland syndrome, which ravages the body every April, rising to a fever come May.

Chris Kamara: 'Plenty of battling Jeff, but lacking in quality' – sounds familiar.

The trouble at this stage and in particular every time watching Soccer Saturday is that one has to sit through every other match commentary for our rivals down at the bottom. Every time there is a gasp from the watching pundit, it could inadvertently affect your club's perilous position. I might leave the room shortly and hope for the best.

Sometimes I wish I supported Port Vale or Rochdale or someone easier than this agony every season…'

…And so another season supporting any one of the North East's teams can be summed up in one extract from the day-to-day diaries that follow. Excitement, entertainment, anxiety, anguish, unpredictable intentions – coupled with a predictable lack of skill, living life on the bitter edge, never allowed to come in from the cold and take a break, take a respite from the frontline action of following football in the trenches, in the middle of a heated dogfight of a relegation scrap and yet the start of the 2008/09 Premier League campaign promised so much in potential for all three North East sides, whilst Hull City were jubilant to be facing the elite for the first time ever.

The season for me began in the oh so familiar territory of Kandahar, Afghanistan with the Royal Air Force. As Sunderland AFC topped their tans in a pre-season tour of Portugal, I was trying my best to shy away from the desert sun, as well as stray mortar rounds, fired from remote hillsides. The European Championships had been on earlier in my tour, but the absence of England from the competition, meant the whole affair was a mere sideshow, to the daily combustion of crucifying heat and choking white dust. A constant reminder of home was not far away though, with a homemade aluminium can replica sculpture of the Angel of the North casting its eye over one and all, going about their daily work.

The arduous 18 hour flight back via Oman, Cyprus and most notably Birmingham – disembarking seriously injured frontline troops, landed in time to see first hand, the start of the new football season.

There was a mixed bag of results in pre season for the four most Northern teams in the Premier League. Middlesbrough and Sunderland had strong starts, whilst Hull and Newcastle suffered surprise defeats. City were buoyant though with the acquisition of Geovanni after his release by Manchester City – the Brazilian playmaker clearly thinking he had a lot to offer the Premier League.

Boro continued their great form from pre-season (seeing wins over Carlisle United, Hibernian and Sparta Rotterdam) into the start of the league campaign, with things looking rosy at the Riverside. Spurs were dispatched in the first game back, whilst a narrow 1-2 defeat at Liverpool, smacked of severe bad luck, as two late Steven Gerrard goals sunk the visitors.

Newcastle, after dodgy results at Doncaster Rovers, Hertha Berlin and Real Mallorca, were far from inspired about the daunting trip to Old Trafford in balmy August. It was a welcome surprise for the Magpies then when the away team boarded their team bus home to Tyneside, with a point in their midst, after Martins had broken the deadlock, only for Darren Fletcher to return the favour, minutes later, 1-1 the final score.

I followed Sunderland to the Emerald Isle as part of pre season for what was to be my first taste of witnessing the red and white colours on overseas soil. Needless to say I was a bit miffed at the last minute postponement of the only game I had planned to take in – Shamrock Rovers, in Dublin. A sudden downpour, disintegrated into incessant torrential rain, causing flash floods in the Irish capital and the fact Rovers' ground is in the middle of a flood plain, did not help our cause. As the rain fell, the wife and I sought refuge in the nearest boozer, where news filtered through from back home, in particular brother-in-law Al, to reveal we'd all receive refunds for our journey over. After we proceeded to inform the remainder of the SAFC contingent in the bar of the great news, Al phoned back to say he was merely joking. It would be the greatest understatement since MP's expenses were considered a little over the top, to say I was somewhat vexed. I would get my chance to see my football team play away from mainland England only three months later.

This strong pre-season – only losing 0-1 to Ajax at home – whilst overcoming far flung opponents from Sporting Lisbon to Athlone Town, did not flourish into their opening league matches. An unlucky 0-1 reverse at home to Liverpool on the first day back in business was followed by a glorious 2-1 victory at White Hart Lane, as new loan signing Djibril Cisse capped his debut with the winner. Still no consistency was had, with Manchester City thumping Sunderland 0-3 at the Stadium of Light (SOL).

ST. JAMES' PARK

Three out of the four sides would go on to suffer internal eruptions, inadvertently affecting the outcome of the season, whether it be publicly acknowledged since, or not. The first and probably most severe incident to occur came at St. James' Park, Newcastle, at the start of September. Amid rumours of a boardroom bust up with club owner Mike Ashley, manager Kevin Keegan storms out of the ground, having resigned with immediate effect. The unauthorised sale of James Milner to Aston Villa was the final straw in the frosty relationship between Keegan and director of football Denis Wise. Pandemonium ensued in angry demonstrations, calling for the departure of the 'Cockney Mafia' featuring Wise and Ashley. The loss of Keegan widened the divide between club and fan, which eventually reaped devastating consequences. Joe Kinnear was appointed as new manager of the club, which would only last a matter of months, after old health problems kicked in.

The next big name to walk out of the corridors of power in the North East was Sunderland manager Roy Keane. His side having lost a string of games, the 1-4 home defeat to an ordinary Bolton Wanderers side was his last in charge, before walking out on the Wearside club, again after a dispute with new American owner, Ellis Short. Apparently, when questioned by the Texan billionaire as to why the Irishman did not attend the majority of first team training sessions, Keane blew a gasket and did a runner. Perhaps, if one is top of the league, then one can do whatever one likes. Not the case after a crushing home defeat. Ricky Sbragia assumed temporary control, made permanent in the festive season as Chairman Niall Quinn handed out the presents of a substantial bigger salary, following eight goals in two games against West Brom and Hull City.

K.C. STADIUM

Next it was City's turn to feel the discomfort of in-house tension. Conceding four goals by half time at Manchester City, North East-born Tigers boss Phil Brown was left fuming, deciding on handing a half time bollocking in public, on the pitch, for everyone in attendance to see. Some argued that it was a motivational requirement for a lacklustre side, others pointed to the remarkable drop in City's form since this debacle, citing a loss of respect between the two camps of players and manager. Certainly no one can argue with the drop in results since the public showdown, as Hull gradually slid down into the bottom half and beyond.

Boro then seemed to be the only club without any public troubles, however the suggestion that the club was bordering on falling into administration never disappeared throughout the campaign and as quality players were dispatched over the summer and not replaced, this rumour, although never materialised, still smacked of 'no smoke without fire'. Without quality replacements, the Teesiders followed suit of the other three, freefalling into the murky depths of the Premier League lower regions.

Back in October, all things were still considered bright and rosy for our football teams. So rosy for Sunderland in fact that they could afford to send their reserve side on an away day jaunt down to the Channel island of Jersey. This was sweet music to this exiled Sunderland fan, living in deepest Wiltshire, based at Lyneham. The chance of a sojourn to any away ground in my radius was a bonus and Jersey was right on the edge of my radar, if not the wife's. In order to make amends for the disappointing waterlogged Dublin experience, fellow serviceman Jamie suggested I partake in a little kidology with the missus and offer the retort that I would travel across the channel by RAF Chinook helicopter, thus thumbing a free ride over, meaning little or no cost from the mythical joint bank account. On the day Jamie confirmed my suspicions and told of a travel itinerary that included alternative civilian flights via FlyBe from London Gatwick and I was not to tell our lass. One thing led to another and after an intoxicating night out my fun-filled story had attracted the attention of the local press. Angela, the missus, had already cottoned onto a suspicious cash withdrawal from the said airport and a drunken conversation confirmed my faux pas. Two nights on the sofa later and a chance to calm down and reflect, until the following day, when The Sun printed the story in its full glory on page 23 and the sofa was required once more.

And so like all of the teams based up North, I was firmly entrenched in the doghouse. Mine was a temporary stay, unfortunately for the clubs, it was a stretch inside that would last until May, reaching boiling point from the end of April, as we settle down to day by day events, following the torturous football, as a way of life…

Malcolm Robinson

| The Diary March 2009

Thursday 26th March 2009
Song for the Day: Oasis– Supersonic

Sunderland

It's the day after the night before and the night before was ITV's documentary of the one and only Brian Clough. In a quality programme which could have ran all night, such was the fascination in the great man's life, it didn't escape my attention what Sunderland could have achieved with the big man at the helm. Our standing in football, the whole package, would have been different if it were Sunderland and not Nottingham Forest who had won two European Cups under Clough's regime. If only the former Sunderland forward had returned to the club he once loved, as rumoured throughout the years, be it in fables and old shipyard tales, however unfortunately the Sunderland board never had the foresight to appoint the great man, even after guiding the Rokerites' youth team to cup success, whilst trying to recover from the injury which ruined his playing career.

Which only goes to add more misery to the current predicament we find ourselves in. Three points from the relegation zone, with a football coach, not a manager in charge. For all I love the man as a gentleman – Ricky Sbragia is not the ideal man to be Sunderland's manager. For one he is too nice, too quiet and most importantly too depressing. Yet as a coach he is one of the best, but the difference between coach and gaffer – handling the team training sessions and handling the press – are two elements of the game akin to chalk and cheese.

Hopefully we will at least reach the end of the current season with our top-flight status intact. At least the international weekend break, that arrives this Saturday, will serve as a break from the daily anxiety and worry.

Saturday 28th March 2009
Song for the day: Finley Quaye - British Air Rage

Sunderland

A day stuck in the office at work is written off luckily coinciding with a meaningless England friendly and therefore the nause of being at work on a weekend is eased slightly.

It gave me the chance to reflect on fans' forum Ready To Go and the fact that my own personal worries about manager Ricky Sbragia were shared by the majority, well at least the majority of sad people bored enough to inspect an internet forum over a weekend.

One thread caught my eye about the possibility of Peter Reid, ex-Sunderland manager, returning to the Stadium of Light in the guise of director of football, in a last chance bid to motivate the playing staff into winning a football match. The amount of abuse that was met with this proposal was unbelievable. This was a manager who guided the club to its best post-war finish, with two seventh placed finishes in the Premiership and yet one would think the Scouser had managed Newcastle and was the lovechild of Sir John Hall and Peter Beardsley, such was the venom displayed.

He was charged with relegating the club in the 19 point season, when in fact he was dismissed way back in October of that year, and so it seems everything else the club has failed to achieve since. Perhaps even the recession and Nissan's redundancies can lie at the door of the Liverpudlian Thailand manager?

Simply outrageous… people have short memories.

Whilst I admit that Reidy lost his sense of direction in those final months in charge, surely the farcical appointment of Howard Wilkinson and Steve Cotterill afterwards did not help matters that particular campaign.

Newcastle United

Considering Newcastle's current plight as I begin this countdown to the season's end, I feel we must take every positive we can. With that in mind, the fact we won't drop any points this week must be looked on as a positive. On the downside, none of our relegation rivals will either, as it's international week.

So, what better way to spend the afternoon than in my local watching England beat Slovakia 4-0 at Wembley. It was an odd match with Heskey scoring (!) then going off injured to be replaced by Carlton Cole. Cole then got injured to be replaced by Peter Crouch, who himself got injured and went off leaving Wayne Rooney as our only fit striker. The Mackems around me were quite happy at Cole's departure as Sunderland are at West Ham next week and like us, are clutching at any positive they can.

Maybe these injuries will see a return to the England fold for Michael Owen. I still find it hard to believe that Fabio Capello thinks Heskey, Crouch and Cole are better strikers than Owen. Despite his injuries over the last few years he is the best natural goal-scorer England has. Maybe England's loss will be the Toon's gain as Owen can concentrate on scoring the goals that will keep us up, then again, depending on the aforementioned injuries, Owen might well get called up for Wednesday's Qualifier against Ukraine.

Sunday 29th March 2009 – Clocks go forward
Song for the day: The Prodigy – Omen

Sunderland

The meaningless International weekend is given a personal competitive edge, as with the forty five pound winnings I had earlier acquired online – predicting three home wins for Wigan, Liverpool and more poignantly Manchester City (against Sunderland) last Sunday – I place a bet on a mini-accumulator, thus relying on the victories for England, Holland, Italy, France and Spain.

England eventually romped home 4-0 over Slovakia, Holland predictably crushed an injury plagued Scotland, Italy held court over in Montenegro with a handsome 2-0 victory and France scraped past Lithuania, meaning that at approximately 22:30 hours, really 23:30 hours bearing in mind the warmth of the British Summer Time waiting around the corner, I was transfixed, pupils glued to a laptop screen, casting a beady eye for any deadlock in the game between Spain and Turkey.

Minutes later, Gerard Pique obliged and settled my nerves, although I still had to maintain a cool outer layer, trying not to attract any unwanted attention from the missus. A meagre five-pound bet last weekend had now emerged into the final straights of this marathon adventure revealing potential winnings of £295. Not exactly life changing, probably just enough to cover some bills, but certainly enough to have my palms sweating, severely panicking until the final whistle.

Finally, the screen updates displaying a home victory for the reigning European Champions.

A mere gasp of air, like a calm and collected professional manager, was enough to celebrate and a quick check of the online account, just to reassure me I had not clicked on the wrong team in the first instance, in an initial lapse of concentration. The money had been deposited and I now consider whether to grab the money and run all the way to a happy and eager wife, ready to spend the surprise income before it had time to register on the bank statement, or 'invest' the proceeds further on the remainder of the international fixtures to play on Wednesday night.

I have identified five or six potential 'bankers', which in normal circumstances would raise minimal payback on a routine bet. However a £295 chancer will bring in a significantly greater profit. The fixtures in question involve perennial international strugglers such as Andorra, Liechtenstein, San Marino and Albania. How much profit would be gained is yet to be worked out, as the computers at work do not allow employees access to online gambling – scandalous!

Decisions, decisions. My decision will be reserved until the odds are taken into account.

To increase my upbeat, if not ecstatic mood, news has spread on the Sunderland fans' web forum Ready To Go, claiming Newcastle could fall into administration at any moment. This has led to a vast amount of piss taking on the internet, including the classic line… 'If this happens, I will be the first man to have repeated multiple orgasms on the spot!' Genius.

Adding more weight to the story, the Sunday Express are all over the news, displaying huge back page headlines with the phrase 'Tyne Bomb' emblazoned on the paper as the main heading.

A relegation for the Mags, along with further punishment of a minus points total next season in the second tier of English football and things couldn't be sweeter. I will hold back on these thoughts though, until Sunderland's own safety is assured.

Better to get one's own house in order, before mocking others… regardless of how piss funny it is.

I checked the odds of the considered bet. The potential returns are £548 from £295, meaning a profit of £253… just for Russia to beat Liechtenstein, France to see off Lithuania, Holland to overcome Macedonia, Croatia to pummel minnows

Andorra, Poland to trash San Marino and Denmark to power past Albania. Perhaps the Danish game is slightly questionable, but the greedy gambler inside of me is wetting himself with excitement.
The potential returns are good; it is the gut wrenching feeling lurking around, should one of those games finish against my wishes, which is battling for control of my brain.

To enable me to live with peace of mind, I have studied the option of claiming to have won £200 and spend the other £95 on the aforementioned bet, which then brings in potential returns of £185. Couple this with the £200 already won and this brings a slightly reduced prize of £385, however with significant less risk and in the words of a time-honoured game show host – 'Whatever else I do, the £200 will be mine to take home and keep, no matter what else happens.'

A difference of £163 from the £548 stated, but everyone is happy. It certainly adds excitement to an otherwise dour, annoying break in the domestic season. One thing is for sure, this amount of stake would not be wagered on the relegation run-in. Maybe a toss of the coin may help settle things in that department.

Newcastle United

Just like Newcastle over the years, my Sunday morning team The Thomas Wilson WMC from Gateshead manages to raise your hopes then throw them disappointingly back in your face like a manky old dishcloth. A semi-final 4-1 defeat brought our poor season to an effective end, leaving only pride to play for in the remaining games.

This afternoon brought a change from football as I was given the chance to see a different Newcastle play, in the form of the Vipers ice hockey team in their end of season play offs. Unfortunately, they take after their more illustrious counterparts in the football world, taking a 1-0 lead, before eventually crashing 4-2 against Coventry Blaze bringing the season to an abrupt halt. At least the basketball team are doing well… apparently!

Sky Sports reports that Darren Bent is being called up to the England Squad for Wednesday. DARREN BENT! Is he really better than Owen? I don't think so.

Monday 30th March 2009
Song for the day: Kasabian - Shoot the runner

Sunderland

I finally succumbed to a mixture of guilt and excitement and told the missus about our windfall via the bookies. I mentioned the option of re-investing the money to accumulate bigger earnings and after a deliberation of five minutes; the jury returned a resounding verdict of 'no'.

Another plan surfaced to enter the equation, be it with scarce time to investigate fully and that was to place the money on Sunderland's reserve side to overcome Accrington Stanley Reserves in the semi-final of the TotesportCasino Cup, which kicked off this afternoon.

The might of Sunderland's reserve side often highlights the case as to why several of these fringe players are not gracing the corridors of first team selection.

Sod's law decreed that I missed out on the bet, due to bad timing, obviously meaning that Sunderland won 2-0, thanks to two goals from young prodigy Martyn Waghorn. Bugger it!

Newcastle United

This morning's papers are full of stories that Michael Owen's England career is over, at least as long as Capello is in charge. I can't believe that the manager thinks it's not useful to have a player like him in the squad. Even if he is on the bench, you always feel that if you need a goal with ten minutes to go, Owen is the sort of player who could come off the bench and score with his only touch of the game. Maybe Capello feels in Lampard, Rooney and Gerrard he has enough potential match winners. Let's hope so.

As a slight footnote to the Slovakia match, apparently Michael Carrick made history by becoming the first sub who came on for a sub who came on for a sub. He replaced Crouch, who came on for Cole, who replaced Heskey.

Back to Newcastle, all the talk today is about the rumours that the club could go into administration. The talk is that Ashley's failure to sell the club and the credit crunch affecting his sports empire could mean the administrators are called in. If this happens the club could easily 'do a Leeds'.

My mate Smurf believes Ashley, allegedly a Spurs fan, is doing it deliberately just for a laugh. If that were true, which I don't believe for a second it is, then Ashley would have to leave the country, never mind the club.

Tuesday 31st March 2009
Song for the day: David Bowie - Let's Dance (Single Version)

Newcastle United

The only bit of interesting stuff I have come across today is the rumour that Mike Ashley has increased his stake in JJB Sports to 29%. Apparently this is the maximum amount he allowed before making a take over bid. JJB of course is/was Dave Whelan's baby and sponsor of Wigan Athletic. Maybe this is Ashley's way of getting back at Whelan for comments made about NUFC last week, perhaps this could be the way Ashley plans on plucking Steve Bruce away from Wigan as well?

Middlesbrough

There are growing rumours that Shearer could be taking over as manager of Newcastle. The FMTTM message board has been full of them all day. It's now on SKY, BBC everywhere. Although not confirmed yet, my first thoughts are that this must be an April Fool's trick which has leaked out early. Surely?

The other big news today is that Boro have left Errea and have signed a new kit deal with Adidas. Judging by the message boards people are doing cartwheels about this. Maybe they'd prefer to be wearing stripes down their arms to playing in the Premiership next season? No not quite, but it is still amazing how excited everyone is. There is nothing like a brand to create a buzz. I thought our brand was the white chest band…

All in all a bizarre day.

MALC (SAFC)

BARRY (NUFC)

ROB (BORO)

| The Diary April 2009

Wednesday 1st April 2009 – April Fool's Day
Song for the day: Boards of Canada - Energy Warning

Sunderland

Our lass rings at 09:30. 'Alan Shearer's the new Mags' manager…it's been on Radio One'.

Half asleep, I try to stir my thoughts. I suddenly remember the date. Hmmm, so Chris Moyles has chosen Shearer as his April Fool's prank – nice one.

And that was the end of it, until the story gathered momentum and even the Sunderland fans' forums were chatting away on the subject. Yet it was still unconfirmed by midday. All we needed now was Mike Ashley to arrive at Sid James' Park and shout 'Happy April Fools' and appoint the despised Denis Wise instead.

I hasten from watching any reports on Sky Sports News, as I can bet my job that David Craig – the main North East/Official Newcastle United reporter is camped outside Castle Grey Skull, verbally masturbating all over the black and whites. It makes me sick just thinking about it.

Newcastle United

What a difference a day makes, I suppose this actually started around 23.30 last night when my mate Colin texted me to say Alan Shearer was the new manager at Newcastle. I texted back, "What's the punch line?" whilst flicking the TV to Sky Sports News. Lo and behold, it was true.

This morning the TV, radio and newspapers where full of the story. Most of the fans that hang around St James' Park when anything happens were proclaiming that we would definitely stay up with King Al. Personally I have said all along that we will stay up, though it will be close. I believe West Brom, The Smoggies and Stoke will take the plunge into the Championship, probably with us in fourth bottom spot. Shearer could be just the lift any new manager brings and maybe gain us a couple of extra points in the run in that we may not have acquired. I believe we will get seven points from the home games against Fulham, Portsmouth and Boro, along with a point or three at Stoke and that will be enough. Who knows, maybe now we may get an extra draw or two against Chelsea, Spurs or possibly a Villa side with nothing to play for on the last day.

I watched England beat Ukraine this evening, but unfortunately Lampard, Terry and Ashley Cole all made it through unscathed. I was hoping at least one of them would pick up a knock before the game on Saturday – every club needs to be selfish in times of relegation dogfights.

Middlesbrough

Shearer is confirmed as the Newcastle boss, but wisely decides to stay away from St. James' and all the hype. That is what worries me about this appointment. He is no body's fool, April or otherwise. He won't want to be part of a circus, he has joined to do a job and also bag a fair bit of money no doubt, but he's bound to be an inspiration to the players and with it looking more like a three horse race between Newcastle, Sunderland and us for two places (West Brom are surely as good as relegated) this makes me fearful.

I was invited by BBC Tees for their weekly fans panel tonight. Presenter Alastair Brownlee immediately asks me for my thoughts about Alan Shearer's appointment. He confides that when he was first told by Gordon Cox he thought the Boro website man was playing him for an April fool.

When Alastair rang to invite me on the show a week ago, I told him how fearful I was about relegation. I'd ALMOST accepted it in fact. He wouldn't hear anything about the "R" word and talked me through the fixtures, the three wins and odd draw that would see us home. That first draw would come at Bolton he added. I felt a bit better about things afterwards.

Thursday 2nd April 2009

Song for the day: Primal Scream - Cant Go Back

Sunderland

Shearer is the new gaffer up the road and Iain Dowie is his assistant. All I can say is that Sunderland fans best concentrate on our own survival and ignore the goings on at the circus up the road, no matter how tedious it becomes in the media.

George McCartney pulled out of Northern Ireland's game with Slovenia in the first half last night. Hopefully, without sounding callous, his injury will at least last until Saturday, allowing a stronger line up of Bardsley, Ben Haim, Ferdinand and Danny Collins in defence at Upton Park.

To round things off, I decide against betting all my winnings, instead opting for a meagre bet of £10, but this time including a win for the Germans in Cardiff, a victorious home side at Wembley versus Ukraine and the Italians to out master the Irish, alongside my long ensemble of 'bankers' already chosen. And so after nine games last night, everything has gone my way… up steps Robbie Keane to boil my piss once more this season. Scoring the last minute equaliser for Tottenham at the SOL some weeks previous was not enough; he had to go one better and bollocks my bet up, once again in the 89th minute, levelling the score at 1-1 for the Republic, which became the final outcome, seconds later.

Perhaps Sir Niall Quinn can show me the way with the bookies, come the Grand National on Saturday. Irish Invader sounds good to me. Here is to an Irish Mackem Invasion at West Ham on Saturday too.

Newcastle United

Shearer has announced that he will be in charge for the remaining eight games only. Of course Glenn Roeder and Joe Kinnear started out by saying they didn't want the job permanently, but both soon changed their tune. I'm sure the door is open for Shearer should he do well over the next few weeks.

The afternoon press conference provided the expected sound bites with Shearer and Iain Dowie officially unveiled as the management duo to pull us out of the proverbial mire. Shearer made a point of saying how this shouldn't be made into a big Alan Shearer Circus, the team was most important and avoiding relegation is paramount. A short spell on the famous St James's Park steps posing for photos followed, whilst the ever-present gang of truanting kids and unemployed locals chanted "Shearer Shearer" and waved mobile phones.

I think there can be no doubts that Al is doing this for the good of the team, but I'm also sure that there are some pretty big bonus cheques going to be dished out when the Toon avoid relegation. Notice I said when, not if. Let's hope this statement doesn't come back to haunt me later in the diary.

Middlesbrough

Manager Gareth Southgate has been visible in the media calling for Boro to be "brave and bold." It is most definitely time now for the players to be gutsy and show they will fight tooth and nail to stay in this division.

I attend an event at the Riverside with MFC in the Community's 'Enterprise Academy' (providing a business grounding for youngsters) where defender Chris Riggott is handing out certificates. Outside I am called on my mobile by writer and Guardian columnist Harry Pearson who tells me that he's been hearing rumours flying around the national media that Boro are imminently going into administration. I said well I'm just outside the Riverside now I'll let you know if I can get through the door. Inside after the speeches and presentations, the way the youngsters are filling their plates I wonder if they've heard the same rumour and are thinking fill yer boots now while you can.

It's always the same when we are struggling that rumours fly around. Urban myths develop. No smoke without fire people say, except if someone just makes it up. The administration rumour and also that Steve Gibson is about to do one will not go away, it doesn't matter how often they are denied.

Friday 3rd April 2009
Song for the Day: Ian Brown - F.E.A.R. (UNKLE Mix)

Sunderland

Today is the first serious time I fear Sunderland may be relegated. The sounds coming out of the club, especially manager – Ricky Sbragia are worrying. The man couldn't inspire a habitual drug user to break into in a factory full of free Heroin. And now his thoughts on the Mags appointing Shearer was to apparently point out that he was glad he did not have to play them again this season. Even if he personally believed this, if he did quietly think that the appointment of Shearer would galvanise our arch rivals, then you do so in the quietness of your own thoughts. You don't big up our relegation rivals in public, before the relegation bloodbath is about to begin.

Couple this with the fact that Sven-Goran Eriksson was sacked by Mexico this week as if to rub salt into our wounds, the Swede could have been on his way to Wearside instead.

The more I think about the dire possibilities of tomorrow and then the following week at home to Manchester United and if all the results go wrong for us, then we will be the ones sitting tight in the relegation zone. Calling Sven… come in Sven.

Our lass is still upset at EastEnders last night and so I have promised her a quick look around the East End when we visit Upton Park tomorrow, although I do point out that the Cockney wide boys of the area, Phil Mitchell and Ian Beale, won't be present. On that note whatever happened to bloody Walford Town FC? Ever since Arthur Fowler departed us, there has been no mention of them. Perhaps they went bust under the ITV digital farce. That would be ironic. And so ever since, the claret and blue has graced Albert Square.

On another note, I see Barry Ferguson and Allan McGregor were banned for life from playing for Scotland today, after firstly drinking in between games and then to go on and give two fingered salutes to the press whilst sitting on the bench was nothing short of appalling. We all swear and do things that are regrettable, but for a captain to do that is inexcusable and something reminiscent from a playground. A two fingered salute to the paying public? I would have stuck them up his arse.

Newcastle United

The Shearer bandwagon continues to build speed, and pressure. The new boss announced that Owen would be starting for the team from now until the end of the season, should he remain fit. That should hopefully give him a bit extra confidence and also put a bit responsibility onto his shoulders. Basically Shearer is saying, 'you are my top striker, I'm relying on you to get the goals that keep us up'. Owen is the sort of player who thrives on this sort of thing, so hopefully he can do the business.

Middlesbrough

We have had a week away from the football after the international break and suddenly I'm beginning to feel pre-match nerves, can we possibly bounce back and take something from the trip to the Reebok tomorrow? It seems like months rather than weeks since our shocking and crushing defeat away at Stoke. We have had time to take stock, recharge the batteries and clear the mind of all the debris of that awful defeat. If we can get a draw it will be a boost and will also post doubts in the mind of Bolton again to possibly drag someone else into the relegation scramble. An away victory would be a real bonus and could work absolute wonders.

The Reebok is not an easy place to get maximum points. In fact it is over 20 years since we've returned from Bolton with a victory. Gary Megson might not be popular with his own supporters but from an outsider's point of view he appears to have them well drilled and playing a physical, direct game not light years away from Allardyce's methods and how successful was that for Wanderers?

It was Bolton's shock win at the Riverside in November which started our alarming slide down the table. Our away fans had just been thrilled by a victory at Villa and a draw at Everton. Match of the Day 2 had praised us for our pace and industry and a European challenge seemed to be on the cards, then Bolton blasted us out of orbit and we have struggled against gravity ever since.

We owe them tomorrow and with 1,700 plus travelling fans we won't be shy of support, surely this can be another turning point in our season?

Saturday 4th April 2009

Song for the day: The Delays - Lost In A Melody

Newcastle United

The day dawns with a new sense of optimism among Toon fans. The only problem I see is despite the new boss, and the new feel-good factor, the players running out at SJP today are the same ones who have got us into the bottom three. Shearer may be in the dug out, but he won't be out on the pitch and therefore his influence on the game has its limits. I wonder how many people have suggested he signs back on just in case we need a goal with quarter of an hour to go at some stage in the remaining games. Picture it, 1-0 down at Villa on the last day, Shearer comes off the bench, scores two and keeps the team up. I don't think Roy of the Rovers even managed that! It's now 1pm. Here's hoping the results go our way today. Big fixtures include Blackburn v Spurs, Hull v Portsmouth, Bolton v Boro, West Brom v Stoke and West Ham v the Mackems. If results go right for us we have a real chance of staying up. If we lose and Blackburn, Stoke, Sunderland and Hull all win, we are in big, big trouble.

NUFC 0-2 Chelsea

The return of the king is over, and it all ended up as a bit of a let down. In the end, Chelsea were just too good, beating Shearer's boys 2-0 at SJP. Match of the Day later will show me just how it came about, but in the meantime the reality of the situation is that we are still in the bottom three; sandwiched by the Smogs below and the Mackems above, a real bad sarnie recipe for a Geordie, leaving a nasty taste in the mouth. Comparing my scenario of doom written earlier to actual results, unfortunately Blackburn and Stoke both won, and Hull got a draw. The game at Stoke next week really becomes massive now.

Middlesbrough

There were storm clouds over the Reebok as we walked into the ground. It had been bright sunshine, but suddenly the weather turned. Ex Premiership referee Jeff Winter told us that Blackburn were losing to Spurs in the early match, but just as we entered through the turnstiles news hit us that a defeat had somehow become a home win. Like the weather, the mood suddenly changed.

The Boro team actually started well constructing some nice passing moves. We were getting right behind our team. Maybe those storm clouds were for Bolton and not for us, however, it all changed in a flash. Hoyte was nowhere to be seen as Ricardo Gardner roared past down our right and ripped in a cross. In-form Bolton forward Kevin Davies, so often our nemesis, left Pogatetz for dead on the back post and finished with a sickening thud of the ball, hitting the back of the net.

We actually clawed our way into the game with a brilliantly constructed goal that showed the class of Alves (and Tuncay) in the set up and a consummate finish from O'Neill. Perhaps it should have been the other way around. We were euphoric in the away end, level again just before half time, this was something to build on at last. Visions flashed through my mind of us making a great escape, then it all went wrong.

There was already a disaster in the making when Pogatetz, the captain, limped off a couple of minutes earlier. (As it turned out we would never see him again this season). Losing an experienced defender and club captain is a big blow indeed.

Then came the equaliser, a goal that seemed to happen in complete slow motion. A hopeful punt into the box from a free kick was not dealt with even though we had several chances to clear our lines. Just get it kicked man. Row Z, anywhere will do. No one seemed to want to take charge of the situation, eventually Bolton defender Gary Cahill stepped up to score.

That was a kick in the bollocks on half time that rocked us all back on our heels. The second half saw Wanderers just score and score again, as we piled forward they just picked us off on the break. In the end it was 4-1. We were routed. We looked down and probably out. The mood was now every bit as dark as those clouds.

Sunday 5th April 2009
Song for the day – Cosmos – Take Me With You

Sunderland

My eyes are aching; I'm too exhausted to think straight, after a day of carnage in central and east London. A mixture of emotions ransack my mind – depression, anger, exhaustion, happiness, they are all present vying for the main stage, to be the star performer, the star turn. After over nine hours in the capital, in what can only be described as an excerpt from The Prodigy's Smack My Bitch Up video, I can no longer function normally. This after a gruelling 12-hour shift at work, all day today, as further punishment.

Therefore I am to postpone my views until tomorrow, half out of tiredness, half in denial about the dross that was served up at Upton Park yesterday just didn't happen. Hopefully the yellow bar will appear on Sky Sports News at any moment stating that Ricky Sbragia has departed from Sunderland AFC – something that will be of a relief to everyone concerned, including the manager himself.

Newcastle United

Speaking to some lads at both the Newcastle and Sunderland matches yesterday tells me a worrying fact. The 'hotbed of soccer' is very worried, as both sets of supporters do not seem to have any confidence in their teams' ability and neither would be surprised to go down. The Smogs are doomed already, so it seems and the only chance either Newcastle or Sunderland have of staying up is if Hull continue in freefall.

Middlesbrough

Before yesterday's game I had an emotional meeting with Jean Thomasson, a long time subscriber, friend and contributor to Fly Me To The Moon, despite being a Bolton fan. We wondered when we might meet again. She offered me some crumbs of comfort about Gary Megson not being popular, his position was tenuous and add a little pressure and it might crack apart, just like Boro.

Sadly I don't think I will be seeing Jean for a while.

I wrote some of the following on the *fmttmboro.com* website –

'Well, that's that then near enough, just the last knockings to go before life in the Championship. All right, there are still seven games to go. We actually scored a goal and a good goal at that, but after inching our way back into the game we threw it away with truly pitiful defending. And how many times have we seen that this season? Yes we could win the next two home games to salvage a little hope going into the final month but how little confidence is now left for players and fans alike?

Even if the ability is there; IF, how can we possibly expect the team to bounce back to a victory and then back it up with a second win. No, let's face it, hope is all but extinguished now. We might as well make the most of what we have left. We said goodbye to the Reebok today and the final grand tour will now take in Arsenal and West Ham on the way. But maybe just maybe we can gain a tiny amount of satisfaction from taking Shearer's Newcastle down with us at St. James' next month, although I don't know whether that is anything to shout about.'

At the end of the game there was anger, there was dejection and there was resignation in the away end. It's been a brilliant ride in the top flight but it looks like the end now.

Monday 6th April 2009
Song for the day – Emergencey Broadcast Network – 3:78

Sunderland

My hopes and dreams of a 'breaking news' story on Sky Sports News vanish immediately, as soon as I switch on the TV, well after a false alarm anyway. 'News on a managerial front now...' the presenter says... only for the announcement that Brian Kerr - ex-Republic of Ireland gaffer - is to take over at...the bloody Faroe Islands! Thus dashing any hopes that it was the Stadium of Light from where the breaking news story had arose – not that I want Kerr to replace Sbragia.

I've had time to reflect on Saturday's events at West Ham. In what proved to be a colossal day out, we were once more let down by the inept attitude of the players and the man in charge of them. A 2-0 defeat to West Ham, sitting pretty in the top half of the league can be overlooked and forgiven in normal circumstances. However, when a manager plums for one up front when his club is in the thick of a relegation battle, then proceeds to play the wrong system and players against a Hammers side devoid of its own best players, fielding a virtual youth team, then one has got to be slightly perturbed, in fact absolutely pissed off with the whole scenario.

Usually, I would take some positives out of a defeat, but none were evident on Saturday. Players not trying, under performing, wrong tactics (again), not a sniff of a clear-cut chance, lack of passion – all the form of relegation material. I could write a book on the numerous mistakes the club has made over the years, yet I could reserve two or three chapters for this season alone and that is not having a derogatory pop at Niall Quinn, after all he has done for my club and home city. It could all be rectified with the possible instigation of someone like Peter Reid to at least motivate the side to victories over Hull and West Brom.

I may burn my ticket for the forthcoming Man United match on Saturday. No, no, I am doing an injustice to myself; I will go and at least 'enjoy' the qualities of Rooney and Ronaldo, as they both go on to secure two hat tricks each.

And yet the day out in London against West Ham was absolute quality, if not some-times bordering on the ridiculous. Being an exile down South, London games are top of the league, in the realms of the fixture list, with me applying for leave as soon as I know what my circumstances are. The train journey from Swindon to London Paddington had an air of routine about it. After visiting Spurs, Fulham and Chelsea already this season, I suppose the shine of travelling to the Smoke is taken away, when the alien journey becomes somewhat routine. The form of the team makes the travelling fan think twice before stepping on board the carriage; does he really want to put himself through the angst and torture awaiting him at the final destination? I overcame this fear, determined to enjoy the final away day in London, the visit of the usual haunts of Leicester Square were on the cards, as was a trip to Liverpool Street to meet the rest of the lads, already by now a force in numbers and unsurprisingly making themselves heard around the local streets.

On arrival back from the pub to the tube at Liverpool Street station, sounds of 'Red and White Army' bounced off the walls, as did fists pounding off the side of a stationary train, now used as a temporary drum by a few inebriated daft lads, keeping the beat of the tune in check. Eventually after much clowning around, we were allowed onto the train, as a new song hit the airwaves.

To the tune of 'I Love You Baby' by Frankie Valli:

Oh Kieran Richardson, you are the love of my life,
Oh Kieran Richardson, I'd let you shag my wife,
Oh Kieran Richardson… I want curly hair too!

This caused much amusement, (although I did refrain from joining in certain parts in front of the missus), as did other songs related to the Mags' new manager Alan Shearer and much-maligned sexual pervert Josef Fritzl. I'd never seen such pandemonium at such close quarters as on that tube and I've seen many incidents throughout the years. Sunderland simply took over the London Underground, the train carriage rocking from left to right, nearly reaching its breaking limits on the hinges, just about staying on the rails intact.

Hammers' fans avoided our carriage at all costs, as we pulled in at several stations along the way to the ground. Chants of 'You can stick yer fucking bubbles up yer arse' echoed around the place in tribute to West Ham's own anthem – 'We're forever blowing bubbles'.

They were to have the last laugh though at the end of the day and although events all through the day often bordered on confrontational, no trouble was had between the two sets of fans and it remained amicable, as it did on the pitch, Sunderland cordially inviting three points onto West Ham's league total so far accumulated this season.

We left the football crime scene once again lauding the fact that if only the players displayed one ounce of the fans' passion, we'd be grateful. I would swap eleven nut cases from that tube carriage for the eleven so-called 'stars' for Saturday's game with the Champions - Manchester United - at the SOL.

I have seen better players down Marley Pots on a Saturday afternoon/Sunday morning.

Newcastle United

So, we begin the week with the bottom of the table looking like this:

POS	TEAM	PLAYED	GD	POINTS
11	SPURS	31	+1	38
12	BOLTON	31	-9	37
13	STOKE	31	-16	35
14	BLACKBURN	31	-15	34
15	HULL	31	-17	34
16	POMPEY	30	-14	33
17	MACKEMS	31	-12	32
18	NEWCASTLE	31	-15	29
19	SMOGGIES	31	-24	27
20	BAGGIES	31	-31	24

Not great I must say. It's also Champions League quarter finals week, which a few years ago would have been an achievable goal for Newcastle, now it is avoiding the Championship league, how the almost mighty have fallen.

Middlesbrough

I was on BBC Look North tonight in a pub in Shincliffe, Durham, midway approximately for the invited guests, a Newcastle, Sunderland fan and I. We each took turns answering the questions from presenter Jeff Brown, while a few regulars looked on from the bar. It is a mixed crowd up there, as far as clubs are concerned, however Jeff confided to me that they were split between Newcastle and Sunderland, no one claimed to be a Boro fan. With this fact in mind I felt a little vulnerable wearing my Boro colours, although Shincliffe is hardly the Bigg Market or Sunderland City centre. Anyhow, we were each asked our predictions on who would go down. I would be last up. What kind fellas they were with their predictions. When Newcastle fan Steve Wraith didn't even mention Middlesbrough in his list of the damned I had to pounce. "I reckon it will be West Brom, Sunderland and Newcastle, I hope." I then raised crossed fingers to the camera.

I exited the pub quite quickly, gone in a flash.

Tuesday 7th April 2009
Song for the day: Empire of the Sun – We Are The People

Sunderland

Someone needs shooting in Sunderland AFC's PR department. Never ones to cover themselves in glory at the best of times, they have allowed the idiot in charge of the team to speak to the press, stating he thinks the current Sunderland squad lack Premiership quality. It may be true Ricky, but you do not go shouting it from the fucking rooftops! Jesus! Cue a downward spiral in the team's already dented morale.

In stark contrast the Mags have held an open training session today in front of 7,500 fans, as Shearer hopes to promote a united front with fans and team… I would say I hope we are taking note, but it's too late. Although I hate to admit it, this could be a cunning plan by Shearer.

Newcastle United

Today Newcastle hosted an open training session at St James's Park, to give the public a chance to watch the lads for an hour or so. An incredible 7,500 people turned up! Can you imagine any other club in the country getting 7,500 people turn up to watch a training session? How many clubs in the league would be happy with that for an average match day crowd? The Smogs don't get much more than that for league games, and they are in the Premier League (for a couple of months anyway!).

On a positive note, for me anyway, my Sunday side won 5-1 this evening. Though I don't play anymore (after retiring at the same time as Shearer), I was there watching and was surprisingly pleased with the performance. A similar score against Stoke on Saturday will do me nicely.

Middlesbrough

Good news and bad news – Pogatetz hopefully only out for one game, Riggott and Digard are on the way back. It is just as well, as the BAD news is that Gary O'Neill is now suspended for two weeks. At this rate we'll be struggling to even get a team out against Hull.

Wednesday 8th April 2009
Song for the day: Northeast – A Ticket for the Game

Sunderland

We make the long trip up to the North East, ready to spend some quality time with family and to take in the Manchester United game at the SOL on Saturday. It is never an easy journey to make. Lyneham, Wiltshire to Sunderland, Wearside, the winding irritating country 'A' roads that cut through the Wiltshire countryside, then Oxfordshire greenery, making way for the combustion and calamity through Birmingham's camera enforcement zone, gracing the annoying road works and 50 mph restricted areas on the M1 – the very same areas where bulldozers and men stand idle for miles, leaving me left to wonder why I pay my road tax?

The sight of Penshaw Monument though warms the heart and eases the back pain endured sitting crumpled like a paper ball for six whole hours.

This journey is made slightly worse when finding out via text message that Sunderland's game at Portsmouth, originally scheduled for Saturday 16th May, has been moved to the following Monday night to accommodate the annoying TV channel that is Setanta.

The fans are yet again second choice to the green lure of TV money. It is bad enough to travel to the south coast on a Saturday from the North East and likewise for Pompey fans in the opposite direction, but on a Monday night? It is a disgrace, especially now I have leave booked, which will need to be altered, whilst it is only good fortune that no travel arrangements have been planned, probably not the case for other fellow Sunderland fans, who will by now have booked hotels and the like. Modern football displaying the growing distance it has developed between the hierarchy and the bread and butter – the supporters.

Newcastle United

Champions League action today, with Chelsea coming out on top at Liverpool. To show how far we are behind teams like these now, Liverpool beat us 5-1 at SJP not so long ago and Chelsea tanked them 3-1 at Anfield. Will we ever reach the dizzy heights of the mid nineties to early noughties again? Not for a very long time I think.

Not much else to say really.

What do you call a Mackem in a suit?
The defendant!

Middlesbrough

A huge boost today as the rumour is confirmed that Didier Digard is back over from France and hoping to be available soon. Get in.

Thursday 9th April 2009

Song for the day: Pink Floyd – Wish You Were Here

Sunderland

A wander down to the SOL in glorious April sunshine is had and so too an enlightening conversation with an acquaintance who reckons to have inside information that Sbragia will be sacked on Monday and Kevin Ball, former player cum legend will take over, short term, to lift the club inspirationally and preserve our top flight status.

The potential overwhelming seismic defeat against Manchester United will mean an intolerable state of affairs, with no alternative other than a P45 for Ricky. After all what is the point of appointing a new manager before United's arrival on Wearside, the assumed defeat taking the wind out of the sails of the new appointment, before the new regime has a chance to kick in. I like your style Quinny lad.

No, no best leave the sacking until after the heavy home defeat, meaning a new fresh start for THEE decisive home game of the season, the following week versus Hull City. Well this all wrapped up in theory anyway. I suppose it all goes to buggery if we do actually somehow beat the Red Devils.

Newcastle United

Not much happening on the Toon front, but two ex-Magpies were in action for Manchester City in the UEFA Cup. Shay Given and Craig Bellamy both played against Martin Jol's Hamburg team in the Quarter Finals, but despite the best efforts of Shay, and a first minute goal from Steven Ireland, Hamburg won 3-1. Given is surely one of our best ever keepers, certainly the best in my time watching, and I would be happy to see him pick up a trophy or two with Manchester City. It would be a shame if he ended up like Shearer with very little to show in the silverware department, despite being one of the best footballers around. Bellamy I'm not really bothered about either way. He did a good job for us, but wasn't a clinical finisher, and (as is well documented), seemed to a bit of a twat, allegedly.

Middlesbrough

It was Kirk Revival night over at Ku Bar, Stockton - a revival of a gone but fondly remembered nightclub just south of Yarm, the Kirklevington Country Club and the alternative music played there late last century. Boro could do with a revival. DJs Andy Johnson and Grant Schofield were playing tracks from the 80s and 90s while a Dexy's tribute band were blasting out hits in the other room. How we could do with a few Boro players from that era. Funnily enough Craig Hignett was in, shaking plenty of hands and chatting away to all and sundry. Get your boots on Higgy.

Over the course of the night several people came up to me to lament the demise of the Boro. The common consensus seemed to be that it was now make or break time for Southgate. Either we win against Hull or he needs to move on out. That's pressure, and this is the melting pot of the North East.

Interview with Matthew Bates before Boro's crucial forthcoming home games v Hull City and Fulham respectively, taken from Fly Me To The Moon fanzine.

Fly: Talking about the club we are obviously in a very difficult situation at the moment. How are the players taking the fact we are second from bottom in the league with games running out? How do you approach that?

MB: I would say approach it day-by-day, game-by-game. I know it's a cliché but that's how you've got to do it. We've got two home games on the bounce and they're both winnable games. We've got to look forward, not be pessimistic. Be optimistic and hopefully we can get out of the position we are in.

Fly: And really not looking too far ahead I suppose.

MB: No you can't. Everyone will be looking at it and thinking we will be in the Championship next year but as players we've got to just play every game as it comes and as I said we've got to be optimistic and hopefully get a couple of wins.

Fly: We have been focusing on the fact forwards haven't been scoring goals but we are going to need goals from midfield or anywhere really aren't we?

MB: Yes. I know obviously the criticism is right and the fans have got the right to criticise players and the team but I know a lot of people have been jumping on Afonso's back, it's not really the case.

It's a case of the whole squad having to chip in with goals and we haven't been scoring goals from defenders at set pieces. I can't remember the last goal we scored from a set piece. It's not just the strikers' fault, we've got to score from midfield and we've got to score from up front. I know we haven't scored enough up front and we can't hide from that fact but it's not just the strikers that aren't scoring it's everyone.

Fly: Were you disappointed at the ref sending you off in the last home game (v Portsmouth – Sat March 14th)?

MB: It was a difficult one; obviously the first one was a booking, I've got to admit that. The second one the ball is played across to me and I just expected to be caught, I touched the ball and expected him to touch me and I went down from momentum.

When I was on the floor I knew he hadn't touched me. I didn't claim for a penalty I just got straight up and ran off. The referee blew his whistle and gave me a second booking. I was still a bit surprised with that but I can see why he booked me I suppose. If I had been in a top team I don't think it would have been a booking.

Fly: *It was so low key, you were just running away.*

MB: *Yes it was daft. Nothing at all. It wasn't a dive. That's not my game, I just went down with momentum. He didn't touch me and I just got back up. If I had been appealing for it I could understand him but I didn't.*

Fly: *You hear so often people say that it's either a foul or a dive but that isn't true is it?*

MB: *No it's not. It's all about balance, momentum, expecting the touch.*

Fly: *In many ways the fact we were down to ten men helped galvanise everyone else in the team.*

MB: *Yes it did. I was sat in the changing room watching the game. We almost won it didn't we with Afonso at the end? I was jumping out of my chair. In hindsight it might not have been a bad thing for the team getting sent off because like you say it galvanised everyone, fans and players alike.*

Fly: *I don't know if you were at Stoke but even though they are all about set pieces it is surely disappointing to yet again concede from a set piece.*

MB: *I wasn't there no. But yes it was, Stoke score most of their goals from set-pieces and it's not something new to them and it's not something new to us. We worked on that in training trying to stop that threat but on the day we never... and like I said we've just got to look forward now and try not to look back and look at the next couple of games.*

Fly: *So hand on heart at this stage do you think we can still stay up?*

MB: *Definitely. I was looking at the odds for relegation the other day and it surprised me how low we were to go down but I'm really optimistic. We've got big games coming up and they are massive games and we need to pick up as many points as we can.*

Friday 10th April 2009 – Good Friday
Song for the day: The Psychedelic Furs - Heaven

Sunderland

More rumours are circulating in the Mill View Social Club tonight that Sbragia is about to go and sleep with the managerial fishes and depart SAFC rather soon. The mood is somewhat upbeat before the appearance of the Premiership champions tomorrow, a mixture of excitement (at the possible change around behind the scenes pencilled in for Monday) and a relaxed attitude, a feeling one would take into a pre-season friendly, perhaps based upon the fact many in here already have the game as an away banker. A good omen? Who knows, if the crowd are relaxed then the team are too. I would rather sit on the side in favour of creating a blistering white-hot atmosphere, to leave Ronaldo crying into his Paella. Let us hope that Sunderland perform better than the turn on stage tonight in the concert room!

Newcastle United

Good Friday - could this weekend be the one where Newcastle rise from the dead and lift themselves out of the relegation zone, or will they remain down amongst the dead men? Will Wor Al prove to be the messiah, now he has had a chance to work with the players, and can go in against a team that are beatable, in theory anyway?

The word is that Shearer has been trying some new formations out this week, working on nullifying the aerial threat posed by Stoke. Presumably that means getting someone to stand on Rory Delap's fingers during the warm up!

Middlesbrough

I suddenly realised that I have become so caught up in the struggle for survival that I have completely forgotten it is Easter. How mad is that? I suppose it isn't good news when there is a fanzine tomorrow. I probably should have printed far more with it being the holiday.

I visited the speedway (Redcar Bears) in order to get away from the Boro relegation pressure, but I couldn't avoid being drawn into chat about tomorrow's game. Even here everyone is thinking about the Hull game and just how big it is. I realise I am now feeling distinctly nervous.

We put a grim reaper on the fanzine cover although the joke is that he is just dropping in on his way up the road to Newcastle... Oh the ultimate gallows humour shines through in all this intensity.

There is more bad news, as Captain Pog is now out for three weeks – typical.

Interview with Josh Walker before Boro v Hull City game – Sat 11th April 2009, taken from Fly Me To The Moon fanzine.

Fly Me To The Moon: *Tough times at the moment – do you still think we can get through it?*

Josh Walker: *Of course I do. You've always got to remain positive and everyone within the club believes we will get out of it. I know we are five points behind but teams have done it in the past and we've been looking at those teams and we'll be looking to be one of those, the team that does it this season.*

Fly: *You were obviously not playing yourself but as part of the squad how do you recover from losing like that at Bolton and conceding four goals. Can you bounce back immediately?*

JW: *Well you've got to hope so. We've got a massive, must win game on Saturday. So, we've got to go out there and get three points. If we don't then it's going to be hard but as I say everyone believes within the club that we will get out of it and take that into Saturday and we'll get out there and we will get a win.*

Fly: *We have got these two home games together so we have to get points now don't we?*

JW: *Games are running out and with two home games against teams which with no disrespect, we think we can beat, we've got to out there with a positive attitude and look to get all three points. If we do that there's six points.*

Fly: *So is your message to the fans that you are still in there battling?*

JW: *Of course we are still in there battling and if the fans who have been brilliant all season could stay with us for these next seven games it will give the players a massive lift. Myself, all the players, the manager, everyone will get a lift. If they stay behind us and we give 100% from now until the end of the season then at least we know we've given it our best shot and I believe we are capable of staying in the Premier League.*

Saturday 11th April 2009
Song for the day: Simple Minds – Alive And Kicking

Sunderland

Manchester United at home – my first home game since Bolton Wanderers in the FA Cup back in January. I should be excited, but I am relaxed, most probably the effects of too much whiskey in the gentlemen's bar, in the club last night and my own quiet resentment about today's final result. With this in mind I have instructed our lass to place a 0-7 and a 0-4 bet on Man United to win. In honour of remembering the famous 2-1 home wins in 1990 and 1997 over United (in which Gary Bennett and John Mullin covered themselves in glory, scoring the winning goals) I also ask for a sneaky 2-1 bet for Sunderland to win. I fear that this particular bet may have bigger odds than the 0-7 bet I have placed alongside.

Match prediction wearing red and white spectacles: 1-1
Match prediction tuned into Reality FM: 0-4

Après-Match – The Debrief
Sunderland 1 Manchester United 2

A marginal, somewhat fortuitous victory for United. I never thought I'd write such notes, not this season anyway. 1-2 and a deflected winner at that, however as most spectators heap praise on a gallant Sunderland side, the miserable unhappy sod inside of me still sees past all of that and blames yet more schoolboy errors and hideous mistakes.

Yes it was a 100% improved performance on last weekend against West Ham. Yes we were playing the European and World Champions. Yes United probably had a substitutes' bench worth more than the combined total of Sunderland Association Football Club, but still there were alarming indictments on behalf of players, management and dare I say it, support and if we are to recover and avoid relegation, it is these three crucial elements that need to combine and gel together.

Even though some quarters enthused over him on the day, Carlos Edwards' inability to beat the first man on a cross into the box was extraordinarily glaring and obvious. The front two looked lethargic and lazy as usual, although the remainder of the side battled like bastards – in particular the gladiator that is Phil Bardsley (quite rightly captain for the day), Calum Davenport and Teemu Tainio.

Sbragia's failing lay in his substitutions. The introduction of Daryl Murphy to any football match involving Sunderland would be nothing short of a criminal offence, but to bring the poor lad on against the cream of the crop, before the likes of Steed Malbranque and even youngster Jack Colback is a sheer travesty. The man is simply not of Premiership standard, or at least does not fit into the SAFC team and it seemed that 45, 000 others knew this too, so why not Sbragia?

Then to put the icing on the cake, the Sunderland gaffer introduces Dwight Yorke to the game. Why bring on a holding midfielder and a veteran at that, when one's side is chasing the game? Perhaps he was allowed a cameo five minutes to play with some of his old chums from Manchester, swapping personal memories, enjoying one last hurrah in the sunshine.

At the same time Yorkie was gracing the SOL pitch with his battered old legs, it seemed half of the crowd were leaking out of the exits, resigned to a 'decent' 1-2 defeat. Surely if your team is 0-4 down with five minutes of play remaining, then fair enough, by all means leave, but at 1-2, with a slight chance of an improbable but extremely rewarding point versus the champions? You wouldn't pay for a cinema ticket and leave early… well unless it was Ben Stiller trying to practice comedy.

Being brutally honest, I had accepted the 1-2 defeat myself, regarding it as a fine result in my mind. What has the modern game come to when a fan of the opposition thinks this? The omens for the modern game do not look good.

Newcastle United

A bit of good news for the area – Newcastle have won the National Basketball League for the second year in a row. Nice one lads!

Nightmare. The Smogs have actually gone and won a game, dropping us into the bottom two. We kick off at 17.15, live on Setanta and so a win would bring us back up the table and maybe even above the Mackems. They suffered a creditable 2-1 defeat to Manchester United.

It seems that Obafemi Martins has got an injury and has pulled out of the game. Apparently the club had practiced with a three-pronged attack this week, so that plan has now gone out the window. The best laid plans of mice and Mags…

Stoke City 1-1 NUFC

A very uninspiring performance and Stoke's keeper, former Mackem Sorenson, barely had a shot to save. Typically, our ex-player Faye once again scored against us, just as he did at St James' Park. Replays showed that the corner, which led to the goal, should have been a goal kick, but in these situations you still have a job to do and defend, we didn't.

Shearer bravely left our only ever present this season, Curly Collocini on the bench and went with a sort of three man back line, with Owen and Ameobi up front since Martins dropped out. Ameobi though was ineffective up front and to blame for the Stoke goal and was replaced by Carroll, who thankfully popped up with the equaliser and the point gained took us back above Middlesbrough, and to within two points of Sunderland.

POS	TEAM	PLAYED	GD	POINTS
11	MAN CITY	32	+5	38
12	BOLTON	32	-10	37
13	STOKE	32	-16	36
14	POMPEY	31	-14	34
15	HULL	32	-19	34
16	BLACKBURN	32	-19	34
17	MACKEMS	32	-13	32
18	NEWCASTLE	32	-15	30
19	SMOGGIES	32	-22	30
20	BAGGIES	32	-31	25

Middlesbrough

This was it then, the big day and wouldn't you know it we won. What tension in the second half, there was a great reception for Hull's former Boro skipper George Boateng with much of the Boro ground singing about him being indestructible, our version of Spandau Ballet's Gold. Did his eyes mist over Donald Bradman style? His terrible error right down in front of the North Stand gifted Marlon King with the match clinching goal, the whole ground erupted once again, "You are Boat-eng… you're indestructible." You have to be cruel to be… cruel.

After the game I watched Newcastle versus Stoke City. Nightmare. After being ripped apart for the first hour Newcastle hit back in the second half and equalised through the appallingly coiffured substitute Carroll. I well remember beanpole Andy Carroll destroying our reserves a couple of years ago. I thought Newcastle might have thrown him out by now; they tend not to have much faith in their teenage talent and now he looks quite capable of scoring a lot of goals, damn.

Sunday 12th April 2009 – Easter Sunday

Song for the day: The Stranglers – No More Heroes

Sunderland

I'm still fuming at the fact the Mags managed a draw at Stoke last night, this after receiving a first half battering from the home side. I was in fact more enraged at this than my own side's failings earlier in the day. To cap it all off, the Smoggies' win over Hull leaves us only two points above both North East rivals.

I still draw hope from the fact that six teams are still embroiled in the fight for the remaining last two drop places. Saturday's game with Hull is now one of the biggest games in my club's recent history.

I console myself with a walk down to Seaburn beach in sublime Easter weather, only to return home looking like a Roker lighthouse red beacon, raw with sunburn. Who'd have thought it, travel up north for the Easter break and end up like a lobster? Happy fucking Easter!

Newcastle United

No matches on today that affected us to any extent. Everton drew with Villa, which in a roundabout way could affect us on the last game of the season. If Villa are already qualified for the UEFA Cup, (or Europa League, or whatever it's going to be called), then we may have a slightly easier game than if they have not. Hopefully we will be safe by then having won our previous five games in a row, so it won't matter. Unlikely, but we live in hope.

Middlesbrough

What a difference a win can make. I played at Darlo with my band Shrug and a band on the same bill, Lifetime Skiver told me about the horrendous problems at Darlington FC; the perils of lower league administration. That puts things in perspective. I discuss Boro with a couple of people after our gig, there's never much escape from relegation, but at least some optimism has crept in now. Then it's over to Stockton to watch Idiot Savant whose guitarist Nathan Stephenson puts his views across about Boro. We all have renewed hope that we can now climb out of this hole… please God!

Monday 13th April 2009 – Easter Monday (Bank Holiday)

Song for the day: Vitalic – Poney Part 1

Sunderland

We retrace the long journey back to the South West, with rumours of Ricky Sbragia's imminent departure ringing in our ears. Alan Curbishley is the latest out of work football manager to be linked with the SOL hot seat.

Newcastle United

Good news. I popped into my local today, and there was a newspaper with the remaining fixtures for all the bottom clubs. I therefore sat and took a guess at how many points each team would pick up in each fixture, and if I am correct, the final table will look like this:

	TEAM	CURRENT POINTS	PREDICTED POINTS
	BLACKBURN	34	42
	NEWCASTLE	30	38
	SUNDERLAND	32	36
R	HULL	34	35
R	MIDDLESBROUGH	30	31
R	WEST BROM	25	27

So there you have it. No need at all for Newcastle or Sunderland to panic. Safe as houses. Shame about the Boro though, but in every battle you get collateral damage. I'm sure they will be back in a year or two.

I'll copy this table at the end of the campaign and put actual points in and see how completely wrong I am. No wonder I never win on the Thomas Wilson FC Football Forecast!

Middlesbrough

Now that I've finally realised it is Easter Bank Holiday I decide to take the day off, well mostly. I go for a walk on the Moors in the bright sunshine where the police are making hay picking off motorists parked illegally in the lay-by near the over-crowded beauty spot, the sheep wash.

I'm on BBC Tees with Bob Fischer's show tonight with Elvis! And the Beatlemanicas, who perform a song together – spooky. We talk Boro, just for a change. After the great result we all wonder if we can escape. Too many "Suspicious Minds," but the Beatlemaniacs think the Hull result will "Help" our cause no end – every pun intended!

Tuesday 14th April 2009
Song for the day: Zero 7 – I Have Seen

Sunderland

A day at work is spent trying to envisage future travel arrangements for the Portsmouth away game, now revised for Monday 18th May, due to television. It is not looking good, as no trains are available without an overnight stop. Our lass has the car for work and so I will require a lift off someone. This is the trouble I have and I only live two bloody hours away. I can only imagine the logistical nightmare this alteration of kick off times has caused for the natives back home. Maybe one day the game may return to the fans, in the meantime we will merely have to live with Sepp Blatter's football circus show.

Newcastle United

All the media focus is on the Champions League matches over the next couple of days. Liverpool, trailing 3-1 from the first leg against Chelsea almost produced a thrilling come back, but in the end the game finished 4-4 on the night. The game brought back memories of Newcastle's two epic matches against Liverpool in the 90s, with both games ending 4-3 to the Reds. The ebb and flow of the match was very reminiscent of the first of our 4-3 defeats with the lead swinging back and forth. Chelsea it is who go on to play Barcelona in the semi final.

Middlesbrough

The fmttmboro.com message board has really changed since last week. What a difference a win makes. Hope springs eternal once again it seems.

Wednesday 15th April 2009
Song for the day: Edward William Elgar - The Nimrod (taken from Enigma variations)

Sunderland

The Sunderland reserves won their prospective league last night with a 3-0 win over Manchester City's second string. Perhaps these players should be selected to play on Saturday in the massive game with Hull.

Today though is not a day just about events on the pitch, but also the incidents off it. Today marks the 20th anniversary of the Hillsborough disaster, in which 96 Liverpool fans lost their lives at a football match. It reminds us all that sometimes, there is more to life than football, even though the Merseyside club's famous manager Bill Shankly would famously say otherwise.

I remember the day itself quite clearly. As a nine year old, I was brought up on a combination of Everton and Sunderland, my father hailing from Wallasey, set in the Wirral, Cheshire and my mother born and bred in Castletown, Sunderland. As a result, the success of the late eighties Everton side tended to outshine the mundane efforts of Lawrie McMenemy (also known as Lawrie MackemEnemy for his sporting crimes on Wearside) and co. in the eyes of this youngster, even though the regular plod to Roker Park was religiously endured.

Everton were playing Norwich City that day, as Liverpool entertained Nottingham Forest at Sheffield. I was at home frantically listening to the Toffees' semi final game at Villa Park. It was only when Des Lynam appeared on Grandstand to reveal there were tragic events unfurling at Hillsborough, did we all sit up and take notice.

It was eventually established that none of my dad's side of the family were present at the fateful game (half of the Robinson side of the family were Red, half were Blue) via a few landline calls (no mobiles in those days). And yet my relatives could have easily attended the game had it not been for circumstances of fate, thus bringing home the harsh reality of it all, even then at a young age.

I also recall Sunderland's very own memorial service a week after the tragedy in a game where we hosted Shrewsbury Town in the Second Division. The match kicked off at 3.06pm, as did every other game in the country, a note of the time the Hillsborough game was abruptly halted. A mark of respect for the fallen that day.

My dad bought us both Main Stand tickets for the Shrewsbury game, allowing us to view the service before the kick off much more clearly and therefore paying our own respects to the 96, who could have easily been any person in the street, as football grounds those days were walking health and safety disasters, just waiting to happen. It was ironic that we spent that game in the comfort of seats – an aspect of the game, through the events in Sheffield, that saw the Taylor report implement safe all-seater stadia at English football's highest playing levels.

Newcastle United

Services of Remembrance were held at Sheffield, Nottingham and 30,000 turned up at Anfield. Two minutes silence was held at 3.06pm in memory of the 96 football fans that died that day at the Liverpool v Nottingham Forest FA Cup semi final.

This turned out to be a day that changed English football, or specifically, the way people watched English football. The Taylor Report following the disaster brought about the introduction of all-seater stadia in England, removing terracing and the cages at the front of stands, which caused much of the problems at Hillsborough.

When I first started watching football at Newcastle around 1984, St James' Park consisted of the huge (or so it seemed) East Stand, the old wooden Milburn Stand, the tiny Leazes End, where the away support was caged and the Gallowgate End where I used to stand in front of the fabulous scoreboard. This was all to change after the Taylor Report, and the 36,000 mainly standing stadium I used to go to evolved over the years into the fantastic Cathedral of St James' with its 52,000 congregation which towers over the city today. We could still use a scoreboard though!

Middlesbrough

I bump into BBC Tees match commentator Ali Brownlee. His assessment is that if we beat Fulham at the weekend then there will be only two more wins required and maybe that will be from the last two games of season. We will have to keep our nerve.

There's a club announcement – all 1500 Arsenal tickets sold out already. People are up for this fight.

Thursday 16th April 2009
Song for the day: Girls Aloud – Call The Shots

Sunderland

It seems like Niall Quinn has upset some fans on the internet today by praising manager Ricky Sbragia, even stating that he may receive a contract extension at the end of the season. I wonder if the stress of trying to resurrect Sunderland has played its toll on the great man, or is he playing his cards close to his chest, in turn motivating the club and its players in public, waiting in private for the summer clearout, including the manager. People are becoming anxious.

According to reports, Viduka, Taylor (Steven) and Lovenkrands should be in the squad and Martins could be too. Last season a front three of Viduka, Martins and Owen got us out of a mess over the last couple of months of the season. It would be nice if they could do it again.

Shay Given's chance of a first trophy at his new club disappeared tonight, despite Manchester City winning 2-1 against Hamburg. The Germans progressed through 4-3 on aggregate in the UEFA Cup Quarter Final and so Given will not be needing a new tin of Brasso just yet.

Middlesbrough

The Barcodes' striker Viduka is fit! Typical. We know only too well how dangerous he can be. At the Speedway my mate Sarah tries to convince me of the advantages of going down. It will be cheaper, new places to visit and we might actually win something, in fact we might win.

I am not convinced.

Alan Shearer was on the box tonight mulling over the pros and cons about having to play all their fixtures after everyone else because of satellite TV. It could be a big factor, an extra pressure.

Friday 17th April 2009
Tune for the day: The Killers – Mr Brightside (Jacques Lucont's Thin White Duke Remix)

Sunderland

I find myself pacing the floor after reading various articles about the big game (the biggest of the season) tomorrow versus Hull. Fans, journalists, players, all urging our fanatical support to sing their hearts out for the lads and spur the failing team onto victory. I am sure if we all pull together we will be fine, we just require patience, without barracking the prima donnas on the pitch, just for once anyway.

I should be there in person, but a 400 mile round trip and work commitments dictate otherwise. Some I know are attending tomorrow instead of last week's glamour game with Man United, due to the biting recession and a need to prioritise the importance of such fixtures to the team. Personally, I would have attended last week if Sunderland were playing an Albanian Shepherd's team in a friendly; such is the clamour to see one's vision of Red and White cloth, when on a pilgrimage back to the promised land of Wearside. My guilt is eased in the sense I played a bit part last week. I did consider forking out more money on a mad dash north tomorrow, but I may not have a marriage left to return to.

In order to calm myself down, I switch on my ipod to warm and inspire my inner self to the charms of choral pleasures. I did this earlier in the season, when we were at home to Arsenal. Sat at home down South and with a Grant Leadbitter goal separating the two sides with 30 seconds remaining, Cesc Fabregas pops up to equalise for the Londoners. I was beside myself and sought solstice in an ensemble of classical compositions to calm my anger and to prevent me from punching the TV screen through.

I only had this desire to decorate the TV with acts of violence once before, in an encounter between Sunderland and Man United, a game which saw me trying to head butt Paul Scholes after a rash challenge, whilst playing up the part of the drunken fool.

I listen to the soothing synths of 80s soundalikes Ladyhawke, but my deviant fingers fondle through the play list, selecting a gradual rise in the levels of anarchist anthems, creating the adverse effect to the whole point of listening to the tunes in the first instance. In the beginning there played Ladyhawke, then Royskopp, then The Prodigy, The Clash, The Jam, White Lies and so until Mackem Music is reached on the dial and I pretend I am the Tannoy announcer for tomorrow's game, whipping the crowd up into a frenzy, raising the decibels, ready to roar the team into Premiership safety.

If I were the PA bloke, I would select the following soundtrack of these exact tunes at such precise timings to bring optimum effect...

13.30 – Turnstiles open – Devo – Whip It
13.35 - 14.00 – A selection from The Farm, Inspiral Carpets, The Futureheads, Joy Division, Kasabian, The Last Shadow Puppets, Mylo, New Order, Plump DJs, The Pogues and Simple Minds.
14.00-1415 – Pumping medley of cheesy dance including Sash! – Encore Une Fois transforming into the edge of The Prodigy's Firestarter.
14.15-14.50 – Sounds of Wearside, featuring colossal hits from Mackem Music.
14.50 – Team run out to Niall Quinn's Discopants, after a rendition of Dance of the Knights.

Newcastle United

The sad, bitter outlook of some Mackems has been summed up in a conversation a group of us had at work today. Two of the scoundrels were quite happy to admit they would rather get relegated in third bottom with Newcastle finishing second bottom, than stay up in fourth bottom if we stayed up as well, a place above them. What kind of attitude is that when all you care about is being better than your rivals? Personally I would rather stay up than go down, and couldn't care less where Sunderland finished. My first priority is Newcastle United, not just having bragging rights over SAFC.

It's similar to when Bob Murray famously said that Sunderland would always have one seat more in their stadium than Newcastle. Is that really all they care about?

Personally I believe Premier League survival to be far more important than just getting more points than your local rivals. Obviously if you can combine both that's a bonus, but for me, the bottom line is survival. Nothing else matters.

Middlesbrough

I was distributing fanzines around newsagents and one shopkeeper was talking through all the remaining fixtures – again there is belief it could go all the way and that we can escape, but it all hinges on tomorrow's result. We discuss where our survival points may come from and what exactly would be the best result from the Sunderland/Hull game. Hull is one very worried club, Phil Brown's latest outburst showed that. Sunderland have no confidence at home - you need home form to stay up. I also add that maybe Pompey are still in trouble as well, isn't their game in hand against Manchester United?

Ticket details have been announced for our last two away matches - £45 at West Ham! The cheeky ....! If only they had gone down after the Tevez affair, mind you I wouldn't fancy going to Brammall Lane maybe needing to win.

I still can't bring myself to look at all the remaining fixtures for the other clubs in the relegation zone. Too many permutations, you can torture yourself by studying too closely, maybe I'll allow myself a quick glance if we win tomorrow, maybe.

We have to win against Fulham. The Gazette says they haven't won here in the top flight for 60 years. We all know they never win more than one away game a season, so, is it good or bad that they chalked up a rare win just last week at Manchester City?

'They're playing well' says my friend FW2 – and Schwarzer is in goal. *'We've got to win'* says Southgate… no pressure there then. Digard is back; can he do a Bullard and McBride and resurrect our chances like they did at Fulham last season?

Saturday 18th April 2009
Song for the day: Peaches – Search And Destroy

Sunderland

It's 3pm. Work and money means I'm residing in the South West watching Jeff Stelling and Soccer Saturday, remaining surprisingly calm… well for the minute at least… until I found out Kieran Richardson is on the bench, instead of playing in the first eleven. Still, it is a strong side, the same that played against Man United last week.

It is the first visit by Sky to the SOL in a while, where we will be able to see which pundit is covering the Sunderland game. This may sound a minor bit part, but it can be all too crucial in the karma with the footballing gods. Be it the wrong, ignorant Cockerney pundit that hates the North and Sunderland in particular and one is in for a rotten afternoon. This week the reporter is actually at the ground and a huge sigh of relief is enjoyed as Chris Kamara is revealed as the chosen correspondent. Always a good omen with recent Sunderland games. Kammy loves visiting the SOL, I still remember him joining in with the home crowd in a horror show of a game with Charlton Athletic. The match saw Sunderland score three own goals, to gift the visitors a 3-1 away win. Sickened by the abuse, the SOL regulars sought comfort in a cloud of frenzied euphoria and began a Mexican wave, much to the amusement of the TV pundit. Not to be outdone, Kammy joined in on the second wave, whilst reporting back to the studio. Priceless live TV comedy by the legend himself.

All of a sudden, my heart is pounding non-stop. It's either the onset of a heart attack or the annual symptoms of Sunderland syndrome, which ravages the body every April, rising to a fever come May.

Chris Kamara: *'Plenty of battling Jeff, but lacking in quality'* – sounds familiar.

The trouble at this stage and in particular every time watching Soccer Saturday is that one has to sit through every other match commentary for our rivals down at the bottom. Every time there is a gasp from the watching pundit, it could inadvertently affect your club's perilous position. I might leave the room shortly and hope for the best.

Sometimes I wish I supported Port Vale or Rochdale or someone easier than this agony every season.

'Fulham hit the woodwork at Boro' – Jesus!

To pass the time, I look to see how many away games I will be able to attend next season should we suffer the worst of fates and sink into the Championship. Depending on permutations in the promotion/relegation stakes, I work out around ten clubs I can visit in the South West vicinity. Every cloud…

Kamara: *'Hull are the better side'* – typical Sunderland going the correct way of messing things up.

GGGGEEEEEEEEETTTTTTTTTTT INNNNNNNNNNNNNNNNNNNNNN!!!!!!!!!!!!!

CISSE 1-0!

I go mental and proceed to jump all over our lass to much amusement from our on-looking cats – Samson and Delilah.

Just before Djibril made his mark on the stroke of half time, the phone rang from back home, in a bid to wind me up, as everyone knows I'm watching and that I hate being disturbed when my addiction is in full swing.

Auf Wiedersehen Lads

SUNDERLAND 1 HULL CITY 0 – HALF TIME… it is early days yet though.

It's the second half and Boro nearly score at the Riverside!

The phone goes from the SOL and it's Al on the other end to say we've had a goal disallowed. Apparently Kenwyne Jones steers in an already goal-bound effort in an offside position. I can't take much more.

Kamara: *'Sunderland are playing superb!'* – Kammy goes on to confirm Sunderland's legitimate goal was indeed offside as Tainio was behind the defence, but it stands and I don't really care, as long as it stands. It is half an hour to go and still 1-0.

Kamara: *'Nearly 2-0, but Hull have got better'* – I can feel an equaliser in the offing.

'Nearly a penalty'.… I can't handle it!

And now news reaches me that one of the lads at the SOL has been ejected for smoking on the concourses. It's all going on, ha ha.

75 minutes – still going well.

STOKE 1 BLACKBURN 0 – Liam Lawrence scores to keep Blackburn in the mire.

PORTSMOUTH 1 BOLTON 0 – Belhadj – bollocks! That's them nearly safe. I suppose you can't have everything your own way.

It is all kicking off at the SOL – players are getting a talking to. At last a bit of fight and spirit amongst the lads… keep it up!

I can hardly write, as my hands are involuntary shaking. It was a similar situation to last year, once again glued to the TV set, that time in the murky surrounds of Basra, Iraq… at least this season I can enjoy my agony in comfort and luxury.

Time for one final nervous wee.

Kamara: *'Sunderland just holding on!'* – Ha'way me bonny lads.

Tuncay through the middle at Boro but cleared away – phew! Four minutes extra at the Riverside, but how long at the SOL? Jeff Stelling is rattling off the full time scores, now arriving thick and fast.

Kamara: *'Hull still attacking'* – it's like a bloody tennis match.

Stoke have won – nice one.

'It's full time at the Stadium of Light' – THANK YOU, THANK YOU SWEET JESUS!

BORO 0 FULHAM 0 – another decent result.

POMPEY 1 BOLTON 0 – not so good.

My body is shaking and it will be for a good while yet… time for a cold shower and a bottle of Valium.

Newcastle United

The results today went pretty much as I expected, with the red and whites and the Smogs getting points. As we are not playing until tomorrow against Spurs, Boro's point against Fulham put us back down to second bottom spot. Sunderland beat Hull, which is what I predicted when working out my final league table. Quite happy with this result, because as mentioned previously, I think Hull will go down.

Middlesbrough

Despite creating chances and applying pressure we couldn't win, surely the game is up now. Didn't you just know that Schwarzer would play a blinder? I go out on the night for a friend's 40th birthday and try and forget about everything – but we're all feeling old now. Of course the conversation keeps turning to Boro and the miracle we now have to perform. I wonder whether I will even be able to face up to watching Newcastle at Spurs. We need the Geordies to lose no question of that, but it could make unbearable viewing. It looks like Hull are now in big trouble and with that gap which has opened up ahead of us we need Newcastle to lose games and then for us to go to St. James' and beat them. Sunderland's win will make it very difficult for us to catch the Mackems now.

I saw a fan leaving the Riverside with a Merson shirt on – where will we find another "magic man" to bring us back from the dead men of the Football League?

Sunday 19th April 2009
Song for the day: Don Carlos – Mr. Sun

Sunderland

The day after the shenanigans of yesterday and I have finally calmed down and peeled myself from the ceiling. Now I am quiet, basking in the brilliant sunshine, sampling a victory barbecue. The Mags are on TV in the background and I occasionally afford them a glance at the score, where a defeat to Spurs keeps them second from bottom.

A mate of mine informs me that none of the Skunks are too bothered as they expect to win all their remaining home games. It is this attitude that has got them where they are now.

No one is too big or too good to go down.

Newcastle United

Tottenham 1-0 NUFC
I predicted a defeat here, but still kind of hoped we might sneak a draw. Alas a Darren Bent goal when Harper had blocked but not held Bent's original shot separated the teams. The formation seemed to change as the game went on from 3-5-2 to 4-4-2 then finished with 4-3-3, but only the final one seemed to galvanise the team with Viduka and Martins coming off the bench to join Owen up front. Martins had a goal harshly disallowed for handball, when really it was ball to hand. Having said that, Bassong could easily have been sent off in the opening minutes, so I suppose it evens itself out.

Premier League Table - bottom half:

POS	TEAM	PLAYED	GD	POINTS
11	WIGAN	32	-5	41
12	STOKE	33	-15	39
13	BOLTON	33	-11	37
14	POMPEY	32	-13	37
15	MACKEMS	33	-12	35
16	HULL	33	-20	34
17	BLACKBURN	33	-20	34
18	SMOGGIES	33	-22	31
19	NEWCASTLE	33	-16	30
20	BAGGIES	33	-33	25

Middlesbrough

Can I stand watching Newcastle on the box or not? After yesterday's results it's so important that they don't win but just sitting here in my house it just feels so helpless.

Eventually I listen to the first half on the radio and I am so happy to hear Steve Claridge getting almost hysterical about Newcastle's dire performance. They're only one goal down but according to Claridge on this showing they are going nowhere but down.

I end up watching the second half with my Dad, biting fingernails time and time again as Viduka and Martins come on and suddenly Newcastle pose a threat. How classy is Viduka? How many games will he last? Why don't Spurs stop stroking it around and go for the jugular? Just score, won't you. See, that's why I didn't want to watch it. At this stage of the season one team always wants and needs it far more than the other.

Then comes the big moment. Martins is in on goal. Oh no… he turns… and fires over. Phew! Sorry and all that but Boro's needs must and Newcastle sliding a place below us in the table makes me feel a little better about the weekend. A LITTLE better.

Monday 20th April 2009
Song for the day: The Verve – Bittersweet Symphony

Newcastle United

The usual round of Monday conversation. Mackems making big noises because they won, Geordies filled with despair, and me looking (reasonably) confident as I continue to predict Hull's incredible descent from top six before Christmas to the Championship by May. I've been to Hull on a couple of football trips, (to drink, not to watch or play) and it's pretty good down by the Marina if you are thinking of going.

Middlesbrough

Clem is on BBC Look North – running through the remaining fixtures for all three teams. It's something I've avoided looking at before now. Of course there has been no escaping Boro's run-in. We've seen it looming large all season. Actually, even before the season some doom mongers were talking about an incredible last quintet of games and how they could send us down unless we had the points in the can. Doom mongers or realists maybe?

Yes, Clem is talking fixtures and what is that he is saying? Boro to go down on just 33 points, he can't see us picking more than two draws, against Man United and Aston Villa for the record. As for Sunderland and Newcastle he doesn't reckon they will get too many more either but the odd win for the black and whites and a couple of draws for Sunderland will see them right. The team dropping like a stone - Hull City - will go down with West Brom and us, or so he thinks.

Thanks a lot Clem.

Tuesday 21st April 2009
Song for the day: Neil Diamond - Sweet Caroline

Newcastle United

The talk around the place seems to be about whether Shearer should drop Owen, who is without a goal for a while. The trouble with Owen is that he is a goal-poacher, not a goal-maker and therefore relies on the service of others. With the odd goal in his younger days the exception (take that Argentina!), Owen is unlikely to dribble past two or three players then take the net off from 20 yards. He needs a clinical through ball, or quality crossed ball into the box in order for him to get on the end and finish. Our midfield is currently lacking any creativity, with far too many similar players fighting for the centre midfield spots. Butt, Geremi, Nolan, Guthrie, Barton – they are all very similar in style, more hard working than inspiring. Jonas G is great at running with the ball, but has failed to create many goals, and scored none to date, while down the left Duff is not the player he was at Blackburn or Chelsea. The introduction of Ryan Taylor was supposed to give us greater options at set pieces, but again the hoped for quality has not arrived yet. With only five games to go we need something, and quickly.

Received the following 'joke' from a Geordie.

What's the difference between Alan Shearer and Newcastle United?

Alan Shearer will be on Match of the Day next Season!

In the words of Blackadder, I am pleased I wore my corset, because I fear my sides are splitting.

Middlesbrough

I switched on Setanta in the morning just in time to hear their tipster reading the relegation odds with Boro 1/4 to go down, top tip behind West Brom. Cheers mate, just the pick up I needed to start the day.

Darren J. Gaffney writes a largely Boro Blog http://gafferssportsblog.wordpress. com and also sends me articles for fmttmboro.com. He is actually doing his best to cheer up Teesside with a prediction that our last five games may prove easier than we thought after all. His evidence being that Boro have faired well in our previous meetings with those teams left to play this season. In fact we've had three draws and two wins against them all. The win away at Aston Villa looks more and more astonishing with every passing week and the cup victory against West Ham was comfortable, so who knows?

Wednesday 22nd April 2009

Song for the day: Style Council – My Ever Changing Moods (Long Version)

Sunderland

The jokes and the banter are building over the subject of the Mags' proposed soon to be departure from the big boys' league.

The text messages are on overtime… *'Fucking ebay… I just paid £5.99 for a cowboy outfit for my little nephew's birthday and someone called Ashley is telling me I now own a football club!'*

Shearer reckons their home games will see them survive. I am not so sure. After the long overdue victory last weekend, a wave of hope and newfound confidence in my team has evolved inside of me and hence I have altered my predictions. It's West Brom, Hull and Newcastle for me, to be relegated now.

After a visit to the doctor today, I was told I would require blood tests as my blood pressure was slightly raised. I simply did not have the heart to tell the poor woman that I was in fact a follower of Sunderland AFC and my condition would most likely improve over the summer, when football takes a break. Instead, I opted for the needle and kept quiet, after all I would only be charged with wasting NHS time.

Newcastle United

I had a £10 bet today with one of the great unwashed from work. He seems to be sure that Newcastle will get relegated, and I don't, so I bet him a nice crisp tenner that we won't go down. I look forward to picking this up, as last season I took twenty pound off the same lad. The Grinch (as he is known) bet me ten pounds that Newcastle would drop into the bottom three at some stage of the season and then bet another tenner that Sunderland would finish above New-castle. Needless to say, he lost both bets.

I received an amusing email today, even though it is taking the Michael out of ourselves. It featured a Toon top and a famous Northern Building society with the remark... 'Going down together!'

Hopefully, it will be a redundant idea come the end of this sickening campaign.

Middlesbrough

Waking up to the aftermath of last night's incredible 4-4 draw between Liverpool and Arsenal I'm wondering just what bearing that will have on the weekend's match at the Emirates. Arshavin finished like an absolute superstar. To score four goals away at Anfield and some really spectacular finishes as well simply fills me with dread.

Or rather it would do if it were not for the Arsenal defence. Without Gallas and the keeper Almunia they look very vulnerable at the back. That Fabianski has looked so shaky ever since his error in the FA Cup semi final. Some of those goals they leaked were not clever at all. Could they leave some windows and doors wide open for us?

There was a reserve game last night from which there was bad news and good news. The bad news first, Chris Riggott is injured again. So we are not going to be able to add his experience to the defensive mix anytime soon. The emphatically good news is that Didier Digard came through an hour unscathed and is looking good. Could Didier be our talisman?

Well, one thing is for certain, the amount of times Digard has been kicked off the park this season shows that the opposition rate him as our key player. Could he be the man to lead our fight back from the brink? I hope so.

Thursday 23rd April 2009 – St Georges' Day
Song for the day: Air France – No Way Down

Sunderland

If goalkeeper Craig Gordon plays at West Brom on Saturday it will cost Sunderland in the region of £300,000, owing to a clause in his contract, with the Scotsman turning in 50 appearances for the club. As if £9 million was not enough for a keeper who barely leaves the comfort of his goal line. There still lies a section of the crowd who think Gordon is magnificent. The beauty of football, hey? Everyone has an opinion. Personally, I would rather have Iain Hesford in goal and that's saying something.

I ponder my options for the forthcoming WBA game on Saturday at the Hawthorns. I have acquired a ticket and me and our lass will be up at the crack of dawn to catch the dirty number 55 bus, then the train from Swindon via Worcester Shrub Hill and Cheltenham Spa, onwards to Birmingham New Street station. The only problem with this is the fact that I am working night shift on the Friday evening, meaning a long 24 hours awake come Saturday. Still, brother-in-law Al is travelling down to accompany us to the game, a slice of moral support in my bid to beat the agony of fatigue.

Preparation for West Bromwich Albion

Option 1
Do I clamber in from night shift, delve into a full English breakfast, crack open the four pack of Stones and continue all the way to the Hawthorns with a can at my side, thus turning the day into a painless blur, to ease the anxiety of the match? The downside of this strategy is potentially feeling the wrath of the West Midlands' local constabulary, always somewhat over zealous in their policing of the away contingent.

Option 2
Stumble in from nightshift, knowing full well I will be awake for a straight 24 hours, take it easy, swallow a load of happy 'keep you awake' pills mixed with the mild venom that is Red Bull, stay alert to cheer the Lads onto victory, then get smashed and celebrate like Hyenas on the train home to Swindon. The downside to this notion being the nightmare of watching Sunderland play for a crucial three points in first hand narrative, with the potential for any future flashbacks returning to haunt me in my dreams.

I suppose there are only so many tablets one can take to stay awake and so I'll plum for middle ground theory of standing in between the two options – slightly intoxicated with my senses intact... if that is remotely possible.

Good news arrives in the form that the home game with Everton has been moved once more to accommodate TV. This time it suits me, falling on my first day off shift. Who says TV isn't good for the game? Ha ha! This means this game will be my penultimate 'live' game to enjoy this season. Due leave has been changed for the Pompey away game on the following Monday, leaving Bolton (away) and Chelsea (home) to be enjoyed/suffered whilst in the office at work. The war in Afghanistan, the withdrawal from Iraq and Queen and country will come a distant second that fateful last day of the season... well at least until Premiership safety is guaranteed.

Incidentally, the potential for a relegation party (to celebrate the demise of the Mags and Boro to the Championship, or to severely drown my sorrows if the worst happens and Sunderland depart the big time) is on the cards, as work transforms into 'swing shift' mode, allowing me 24 hours off, switching from day shift into nights. The lads are already one step ahead, sending pictures of Newcastle's new strip for next season, complete with Coca-Cola Championship badges on the sleeves. I'll bide my time first...

I am awoken from my slumber by a phone call from our lass on her way to work. Last time it was the appointment of Shearer up the road, this time news arrives from East Anglia on the appointment of Roy Keane as Ipswich Town manager. After sacking current manager Jim Magilton this week, the Tractor Boys have taken a gamble on the ex-Sunderland gaffer.

I have mixed emotions. On one end of the scale I am disappointed someone else has acquired our man so soon, but reality soon kicks in displaying Keane for what he is – a managerial loose canon. Keane has stated that he saw a great opportunity with Ipswich; it is a pity he wasted the biggest opportunity of the lot, the one he blew with Sunderland. Speaking to a Town fan yesterday at work, I suggested Keane as manager before the news was revealed, to which I received a muted response. 'Maybe he's a bit like Keegan... a quitter,' he remarked. And who can argue with that?

Without the calamitous 80 million he had to spend at the SOL, I personally think he will struggle, maybe not in the Championship, but certainly in the Premiership if they were to be promoted. I wonder how many ex and current Sunderland players he will sign. Niall Quinn should offer him a job-lot sale starting with Daryl Murphy, Dean Whitehead, Russell Anderson, Nick Colgan, Roy O'Donovan, David Meyler, Nyron Nosworthy, David Connolly, Carlos Edwards, Greg Halford, Anthony Stokes, Paul McShane... need I go on? Once the Ipswich fans see the car crash that is the above selection and the waste of a healthy transfer kitty, they will soon follow in the footsteps of the lone fan I was talking to in failing to get too excited over the appointment.

Rant Over!

Newcastle United

The build up to the weekend begins, the tension builds more and more each week and the banter increases. Sunderland feel they are certs to beat West Brom at the weekend and we are in trouble if we don't beat Pompey. Unfortunately we have to wait until Monday to play.

It's St. George's Day today and while I was out in Newcastle in the evening there were a few England flags out on display, but it's still nowhere near as big as St. Patrick's Day for some reason.

Middlesbrough

Alan Shearer was on Sky Sports News this morning talking about the qualities of Mark Viduka and how he hoped the Aussie would be fit for Monday. IF he stays fit and what an IF, Viduka could make all the difference for them. Such a clever player and I well remember some of those astute performances for us in the UEFA Cup, when fed with back to goal he turned and defenders couldn't get near him, he was unplayable in fact.

Shearer also said Newcastle need to win three games; this has to be our target as well. Although they are now below us, our biggest problem is we are not likely to get any of those wins from our next two games away at Arsenal and home to Man United. If we could somehow sneak our third draw in a row at the Emirates and then looking at the way Man United struggled against Pompey last night, who knows? Oh and we could do with Hull and Newcastle failing to win, then anything we could conjure from Arsenal and Man United will be worth its weight in gold. Looking ahead to that game at St. James' Park, it looks more and more like a relegation decider. Please, Mark Viduka, do not make a decisive contribution.

It's looking like the fight is between Hull, Newcastle and us now, well for the moment anyway. Things have a habit of twisting and turning; can we bridge the gap or ride our luck until Newcastle away?

Friday 24th April 2009
Song for the day: Brain Eno – Going Unconscious

Sunderland

My hopes of a quiet night at work are dashed as three aircraft are due to depart early on Saturday morning, thus meaning I will have enjoyed no sleep from 13.30 today until bedtime tomorrow – after enduring the full day out at West Brom.

A similar encounter was had once before after a day trip to Iraq. The venue that day was White Hart Lane, the opposition Spurs in a Premiership game. After a mere half hour of sleep, I dragged my weary body through London, hitting a second wind on arrival at the ground, which peaked with an argument with a group of stewards about the non-sale of alcohol to away fans at half time, finally retreating to a shell of a man on the train home, witnessing a poor display from the Lads and Craig Gordon in particular.

I fear the same tomorrow; perhaps a gentle kip on the train may be had, although this often makes me feel worse. Provisions of vodka and Red Bull will suffice, coupled with incessant popping of Pro Plus pills… aah the joys of following Sunderland and football in the forces. I sincerely hope the players reward my efforts.

On the internet, a few Sunderland fans are recalling their previous experiences at the Hawthorns down the years. They all seem to be positive, which nags away at my football paranoia, meaning surely my first visit to Albion tomorrow will end in a rare home victory over Sunderland. If it is a defeat tomorrow against the league's basement side, then I will hold my hands up as the Jonah of the Hawthorns.

Newcastle United

Heard a good one today. *Did you know that the new series of CSI Sunderland has been cancelled? Apparently in Mackemland there are no dental records and the DNA is all the same!* Boom boom!

The weekend begins here and at the business end of the table i.e. where we are, I predict Hull and Boro to lose, Sunderland to draw with West Brom, Blackburn to beat Wigan and the Toon to win against Portsmouth… fingers crossed.

Middlesbrough

I will travel down to London tomorrow on the train. I wonder If there will be many more train trips to the capital in the future? There's not too many London clubs in the Championship now, not even Charlton any more. What a warning that is as well, the fate of Charlton Athletic. Be thankful our club is on a far sounder footing financially, well I hope so.

This morning on the satellites came the disappointing news that Almunia is back in training and could be fit to face us on Sunday. Not so good for our cause, no doubt about that. The very un Fab Pole is flinging them in his net at present, though a far better rumour is that Wenger might be tempted to play a weakened side with the Champions League in mind. Then again their weakened sides do tend to get to the final stages of cup competitions, yet still, it would be very welcome news.

I was at Middlesbrough in the Community today talking with Julie Sewell of the E2E programme. They do so much vital work getting teenagers back on track in their lives. I hope their budget isn't too reliant on Boro's Premiership status.

Boro fan Harry Pearson writing in his Guardian column today talks about how at this stage of the season you spend as much time and emotion on wanting your relegation opponents to fail as your team to succeed, too right you do. I hope Liverpool turn Hull over tomorrow and West Brom's Boro hero boss Tony Mowbray remembers his roots and whacks Sunderland at the Hawthorns. We'll have to wait until Monday for Newcastle versus Pompey but you have to wonder whether playing last all the time will prove too much in terms of pressure for the Mags, especially if they are constantly playing catch up.

I haven't quite taken to writing on walls and getting the abacus out like Harry to work out all the ramifications, yet there is no doubt about it we need others to keep on losing as well winning points ourselves.

Saturday 25th April 2009
Song for the day: Squarepusher – Hello Meow

Newcastle United

Well, well, well, what happened down at The Hawthorns? Bottom of the league West Brom tank the Red 'n' Whites who were so confidently predicting three points and guaranteed safety after this match. They are really in trouble now and I can't see them getting another point, certainly not a win. Luckily for them, Hull and Middlesbrough won't get another point either so the Mackems should be safe, but only just.

I notice that former Mag Kieran Dyer made his umpteenth return from injury for West Ham today. From what I heard on Sky Sports he is still the player he always was – going clean through at one stage and firing weakly straight at the keeper.

Two big games tomorrow, then us live on Setanta on Monday. The Sunday games see Blackburn host Wigan and Arsenal play the Smogs. We really need the the Gooners and Wigan to win, but I fancy Fat Sam's side to nick a win against Wigan. My other half is away all day tomorrow so I suppose an afternoon in the Usworth Club watching football is in order. It's a hard life!

Middlesbrough

Up early for train to London – making a big weekend of it. Pity match kick offs keep changing and so it ended up costing twice as much. Luckily I was able to get a reasonable fare on Grand Central. Still the authorities never consider the fans. It's the London marathon tomorrow – no wonder I couldn't find cheap hotel space.

I'm sitting on the early train hoping against hope that Hull and Sunderland lose today. If they win we'd be in even bigger trouble. I'm not going to follow either game, that would just be torture. Funnily enough I'm meeting my mate Yvette in the afternoon just round the corner from the London Dungeons, quite apt then?

I just heard last night that Geoff Vickers of Middlesbrough Supporters South and myself are going to the World Cup - we have been successful with three World Cup tickets in Cape Town and Durban. I hope against hope the World Cup will follow another Premier season for Boro. Maybe just something to look forward to even if we do go down… don't even think it.

I bumped into a fellow Boro fan at the Tower of London, we chatted about the weekend's games while some medieval rein actors were showing off giant siege engines in the moat below us. It could feel like a siege for us by the end of this campaign. I must stop trying to link everything back to our relegation struggles, I'm starting to sound obsessed.

My dad sent me a text that Sunderland had lost 3-0 at WBA. Getinthere! Stoke City lost at home to Liverpool. Brilliant. John Donovan (Twelfth Man) text me from a pub in Golders Green – "good results – optimistic now or is it the beer? Time to take advantage." Too right.

Sunday 26th April 2009

Song for the day: Aphrodite's Child – The Four Horsemen

Sunderland

Apparently I must be a Jonah of gigantic proportions, as Sunderland suffer a humiliating 3-0 defeat at The Hawthorns, in easily one of the worst performances I have ever seen by my team… and I've seen some horror shows over the years.

No effort, played like strangers, lack of passion, lazy, bone idle, clueless, no creativity, no leadership, no commitment, gutless… need I go on? Surely after this the imbecile in charge must be put out of his misery, even if only four games remain.

The players currently fall into two categories: The group that are simply not good enough for the Premiership and those that have the talent but can not be arsed enough to care, the mercenaries. Add to the mix a manager whose tactics are quite disturbing – substituting an attacking midfielder (Andy Reid) with a defensive/holding midfielder (Dean Whitehead) when chasing a game is astounding, or what about adding an extra forward to the game (David Healy) with only four minutes left to play and already 2-0 down, it's astonishing.

Even behind the scenes questions are being asked. Craig Gordon – Sunderland's nine million pound Scottish International goalkeeper has cried off the rest of the season with an injury, however it transpires that when Gordon next pulls on the green jersey, it will cost the club £330,000, as he makes his fiftieth appearance in red and white, activating a clause in his contract, in which Sunderland pay even more money to his former club Hearts. Maybe it is sheer coincidence, but with rumours circulating that the Irish based Drumaville consortium still owning 60 per cent of the club (Ellis Short waiting in the wings to take over) and the Irish economy on its knees, means potentially the club is cash strapped beyond belief. When things do not go well at a football club, sceptical ideas like these normally do the rounds. Just what is going on at the Stadium of Light?

It was though, just like at West Ham (and to be fair most away games), still a great day out (minus the 90 minutes of embarrassment). It is the banter, the crack, the merriment, the togetherness and sense of belonging, the random madness of it all. Akin to a mini lads' holiday, if only for the day. Another place, somewhere new and even if one has been before, there is always a new experience to be had. If it were not for this, then away days would have been abandoned a long time ago, as the team themselves have never been consistent enough to merit the effort.

The atmosphere somehow always seems superior, that small contingent making all the noise, but it is a small contingent of passionate hardcore lunatics, that care about their team... well that and the hoards of pissheads on their day out too.

The day never really started, it was a continuation from Friday night's shift at work. No sleep was had and so I arrived home at 07.00 determined to stay awake. I woke the missus and brother-in-law (staying down especially for the game) as I headed for the fridge and a can of lager was summoned. To be fair, Al joined in the blatant abuse of alcohol at this early hour and we were set for the train journey ahead. Swindon to Gloucester, then Gloucester to Birmingham New Street, where along the way I only had the tendency to fall asleep once through my painful aching exhaustion. This one lapse in concentration fell at a crucial moment on changing trains at Gloucester. Al failed to notice me flagging and that I was not immediately behind him exiting the train, thus resulting in a mad dash off the carriage, when fortunately waking up in time, before I ended up in South Wales along with the train. The remainder of the lads were met on arrival in Birmingham and the jovial times began, until 15.00 at least.

Needless to say the team's performance raised major concerns amongst the away end. Some fans were arguing amongst themselves at where it all went wrong, or on the merits of supporting or barracking the team, others just stood in shock at the woeful display on show. Some still chose to mock Newcastle and the fact they are still in the relegation zone. This completely amazes me. We need to look at ourselves before mocking others. Both clubs are rubbish. There is even a picture doing the rounds featuring all of the characters from Auf Wiedersehen Pet, now replaced with images of Geordie icons including Shearer, Joe Kinnear and Ant and Dec, with the phrase 'Auf Wiedersehen Premiership'. One could easily replace it with Wearside images of Steve Cram, Peter O'Toole, Dave Stewart, Billy Hardy and Kate Adie.

The one sad story about the whole situation dawned on me with a matter of minutes remaining at the Hawthorns. I promised myself that this shower of shit would be my last 'live' game of the season, let down by Sunderland AFC once again, as we all have been many times over the decades. I even went as far to suggest that this was my lot with football for now. Players on ludicrous amounts, swapping clubs like stickers in a school playground, without regard for the consequences, living on a different planet. It was only then I asked myself what would I do with myself? What else was there? Yeah music and other sports were fine, but not as addictive as football. It is not even an addiction; it has gone way past that level. It is a habit, part of my life as are the organs in my body. Without it I would not be able to function. And so for all the agony and the upset, the depression and anxiety caused, football is so ingrained into my personal society that I am simply not allowed to walk away. I am tied for life. Therefore, one will just have to make the best of a bad situation. Perhaps I will start my own Wearside football club and call it 'Roker Park Old Boys 1879' or something along those lines, a la AFC Wimbledon and FC United of Manchester. A breakaway fans' team, is this the future of football?

Soldiers versus Footballers

I received an e-mail today from a mate serving out in Camp Bastion, Afghanistan. He too is a Sunderland fan and like me, suffering the loss at The Hawthorns. Having stayed awake (work hours vary out there and they are three and half hours ahead of the UK) in order to catch the coverage via BFBS radio, he feels saddened and let down considerably, by the lack of effort shown by the players. He concludes his message with 'I don't think they (the players) realise how far reaching the effects of a morale-sapping performance are to individual lives around the world.'

This took me back to my time in Basra, Iraq, in the spring of 2008, the Tyne-Wear derby game was pencilled in, slap bang in the middle of my time out there. Despite a gruelling 18-hour night shift, I awoke early during the heat of the day; to take in the big match, live in the crew room, some two miles away. Considering one must carry body armour and a rifle everywhere you travel, this was a ball ache I could do without.

The players rewarded my efforts with a shambles of a display, crashing to a lacklustre defeat to our archrivals. I spent half of the game on the floor of the office, dodging incoming mortar rounds, pounding the tarmac outside. Whilst lying there face down, I wondered if the players on the pitch knew what I had gone through to witness such drivel. Of course they wouldn't know and probably in this day and age, didn't care, yet if they had only put in an ounce of the effort I had done just to see the game, then I would not have any complaints. That is all I ask as a fan.

I visualise the lads perched around the nearest radio or TV, awaiting the final scores rolling in, eager in anticipation of a much needed boost, to drive the inner spirit through another day of dust, sweat and tears. Over in the corner is the Sunderland fan, raging with despair, despondent that all hope is lost, drowning in the hope that one day his time will come and he too will be the top trump of the gallows banter, so often directed at him, through another venomous defeat.

Stick eleven soldiers on the pitch any day.

Newcastle United

Swings and roondaboots, as they say in Geordieland. Boro lost, as expected, but Blackburn won as predicted. That moves them up a bit and puts Sunderland now fifth bottom. With a four point gap between us and Hull, the game against Portsmouth is really important, not just for the points, but from a psychological point of view. A defeat will be followed by a trip to Anfield next week, which will probably mean another loss. That would mean with three games left we would be a minimum of four points adrift, translating that we would need at least a win and a draw from our final three games. Our goal difference is good enough to count as a point if we were to end level with Hull, unless we receive a real thumping from Liverpool.

Middlesbrough

Woke up and the sun is shining through the curtains of my Travelodge room. I hope it is shining down on us today. My thoughts have turned to the season Venables rescued us from relegation. We won 3-0 at Highbury; it was like an Easter resurrection to help clinch safety. What would we give for a repeat today? Or how about remaining unbeaten at the Emirates - if we could record a third successive draw there it could be a precious point.

Not to be this time though – I'm on a train full of knackered marathon runners looking back on how we managed to knacker our survival prospects by a capitulation at the Emirates. We started out okay but without really threatening

Arsenal. Not like the last two years there, when we have gone straight at them and scored.

There were plenty of spare seats in the Arsenal stands; I was hoping that the players would share the attitude of the season ticket holders that this match wasn't worth turning out for. But despite Champions League priorities Arsene put out a strong side.

It was sickening to go a goal down, even more so when we were all inundated with texts from TV watchers at home telling us the goal was offside, worse still that we should have had a penalty.

In the second half there were two decisive moments, firstly Aliadiere's miss. He has twice scored against his old team since joining us; a more composed finish could have totally altered the outcome of this game. Almost straight afterwards came the second killer moment when Fabregas sidestepped Jones who had come rushing out and that was game over. Well, at least it was game over once Southgate removed King for Adam Johnson. It was a big mistake, not least because Downing had been having real success down the right and was now moved inside and out of the game.

So, we lost again and in all truth it was a pitiful display in the end, totally lacking in fight. In the pub afterwards Blackburn are winning, 1-0 then 2-0. Forget it! I don't want to know anymore. I don't know whether I'll watch Newcastle tomorrow.

We desperately need results ourselves but how do we do that when we can't score goals? The only bright spot is that Digard came off the bench to finally play some football, but it's not much to cling onto. It's all on Monday now and looking more and more like we need to rely on Newcastle and Hull continuing to lose.

Monday 27th April 2009
Song for the day: Frank Sinatra – Stardust

Sunderland

No news of Ricky Sbragia leaving Sunderland. The Alan Curbishley rumour will not go away, some quarters are suggesting that he may even arrive as assistant to Sbragia. Kevin Ball still gets my vote. If there is anyone who can motivate the team, then Bally is your man.

My mind is drawn to the Mags' game with Portsmouth tonight. I was somewhat relaxed yesterday (even after the debacle at West Brom), confident that Boro would be easily beaten by Arsenal. This is not the case tonight. Blackburn won yesterday, virtually ruling them out of the relegation run in. Now it is down to five – Sunderland, Boro, the mags, Hull and West Brom – who are on twenty-eight points and are not finished just yet.

I fancy Newcastle to win tonight; then again I fancied our chances on Saturday just gone. I have a nervy feeling that the bastards will win, probably a fluky goal at that. I do not intend to watch any part of tonight's game, not even the score updates on Sky Sports News. Unbearable.

Newcastle United

I was sent an interesting article today from The Irish Times. The article is by a Leeds fan and is called *Does The Premiership Really Need Newcastle?* The basic outline is that he feels upset that people are worried Newcastle might go down, while no one really cared when Leeds did. The writer, Mr Tom Humphries, also pleads Sunderland's case. This may well have something to do with Sunderland's large Irish connection and Mr Humphries' employers. Some notable quotes include:

"This year, as so often in the past, it is amusing to find Newcastle United down there crossing their fingers and hoping for a break. I like Newcastle. I like their fans and I like the people, BUT as a person who has pledged his troth to Leeds United I am always vexed and bemused by the great affection offered to sad and pathetic old Newcastle, especially when I weigh it against the spite directed at Leeds."

"Why is it always considered a disaster for football and a terrible indignity for a great old club if Newcastle have to spend any time with their fat asses hovering over the relegation blender and none of the serial misfortunes visited upon Leeds United is ever humiliating enough to satisfy the bloodlust of those who keep themselves alive by hating Leeds?"

A slight tinge of bitterness and jealousy there perhaps? Make your own mind up.

NUFC 0 – 0 Portsmouth
Despite all the talk of this being a "must win" game, a point is okay in my opinion. It means we are only three points from Hull, with a superior goal difference (bar-

ring a sound thrashing at Anfield next week). To put it another way we are only one game from Hull, whereas if we had lost it would have taken two games to reach parity. I'm still convinced our final two home games against Fulham and the Smogs will give us enough points to reach safety, even if we end up relying on goal difference.

The game itself was pretty decent with Newcastle having the better chances and all three strikers, Owen, Viduka and Martins, having great chances to score. Alas it was not to be but it's another point in the bag.

Premier League Table - bottom half, 27.04.09:

POS	TEAM	PLAYED	GD	POINTS
11	WIGAN	33	-7	41
12	STOKE	34	-16	39
13	BOLTON	34	-11	38
14	POMPEY	34	-15	38
15	BLACKBURN	34	-18	37
16	MACKEMS	34	-15	35
17	HULL	34	-22	34
18	NEWCASTLE	34	-16	31
19	SMOGGIES	34	-24	31
20	BAGGIES	34	-30	28

To summarize the weekend, on Friday I wrote: *"I predict Hull and Boro to lose, Sunderland to draw with West Brom, Blackburn to beat Wigan and the Toon to win against Portsmouth."* Well Hull and Boro did lose, Sunderland lost, Blackburn won and we drew, so I was kind of on the right lines.

Middlesbrough

Should I watch the Newcastle match? Will I be able to bear it? Could tonight shut us out of the running altogether. Surely Newcastle can't be as inept again, fingers crossed they are.

With the game a few minutes old I finally decided to switch on the box. Portsmouth were passing nicely and well on top, the atmosphere was frightening old school St. James', the opponents booed with every touch. By the end of the half Pompey looked thoroughly intimidated, their earlier composure ebbing away and errors creeping in. Martins freed himself and hammered the ball with the goal at his mercy. Over the bar. Phew! He really should have scored; the second half could be painful to watch.

In the second period Newcastle cranked up the action. I switched over a couple of times to the Reading and Norwich promotion/relegation battle in the Championship just to calm my nerves. I could be travelling to one or neither of these teams next season, both have recently played in the Premier League - a sobering reminder of what fate could have in store for us.

Back with Newcastle and Viduka looked ominously good. With 15 minutes gone the commentator was saying he was blowing hard, thank goodness he is not fully fit. In fact looking round the Newcastle side there are a few veterans out there, have they got the legs for this relegation campaign?

Then it happened in a flash, Owen through on goal, I can barely look. Straight at James. Time to breathe again. Viduka off but Carroll is on. Then just as Newcastle looked to be cranking it up they suddenly fell away. Butt had to leave the field as well and by the end of the match it was all Portsmouth. If only Portsmouth had actually been going for the win they would surely have won. As it was they left the big men back for corners but Richard Hughes did hit the post and how on earth did Crouchy scuff that shot? I shouted out loud as he passed it straight to Harper.

Come on... come on referee, the final whistle... Yes, he's blown. We are down to second from bottom again with our appalling goal difference, but with Newcastle having blown one of their biggest opportunities of all. A massive home game and they fired blanks, even going out all guns blazing with Viduka, Owen and Martins. It doesn't look like home is going to be an advantage this time round.

Tuesday 28th April 2009

Song for the day: The KLF – What Time Is Love? Live at the Trancentral (Original Version)

Sunderland

I am feeling slightly happier today; Newcastle's failure to beat Pompey being the main reason for my jovial mood. My predictions so far have been as wide of the mark as Michael Owen's shooting and now I seriously think the Mags will go down... well I'm pretty certain. Hull and Newcastle with West Brom now for me.

In other news, ex-manager Roy Keane is planning to sue SAFC if we stop up, citing a clause in his contract indicating a bonus payment for the Irishman, if Sunderland retained their Premiership status for a second season in a row.

As far as I can see, the miserable bottling bastard lost all of his privileges and rights the moment he threw his toys out of the pram and walked out the marbled entrance at the SOL. All contracts must have been ripped up at this moment surely. It is not as if the bloke is short of a few bob and he is the first to question the morality of modern day professionals, when asking for vast amounts of money himself. It seems Keano has a serious case of double standards going on. This was also reflected when commenting on players refusing to move to the North East region, when he himself never uprooted from his family home in Cheshire. I could continue… the man has lit a fuse in me and many other Sunderland fans. He is in serious danger of tarnishing his memory on Wearside even further, but then do you think he cares?

Newcastle United

It's incredible how much time Mackems spend talking about Newcastle. Whether it's the football team, or the city itself, or anything even remotely associated with the place, it simply seems to be the hot topic. This is not a new thing with the relegation battle, but something that has been going on as long as I remember. The petty jealousy that seems to inhabit some of our small town cousins is sometimes hard to believe. Therein lies the problem I think. A lot of people just can't get over the fact that Newcastle, whether you like it or not, is the big city in the area – the unofficial capital of the region.

I must point out here that Sunderland is not a city. It is a town that has been given city status. This means from an official point of view it is ranked as equal to a city, but doesn't mean it actually is one. Cities have cathedrals. Towns don't. So in the end, whether the Mackems like it or not, Newcastle, Manchester, Liverpool, London, Coventry, Canterbury, Durham, Lincoln and all are cities, while Sunderland, Huddersfield, Gateshead, Cleethorpes, Bognor and Bury are all towns. This should not stop you enjoying your town, or make you jealous of your neighbours – just accept it and get over it. Newcastle is the bigger, brighter, more attractive conurbation, just as Newcastle United is and always will be the bigger football club, whether we get relegated or not. So there! Na na na na na!

Thinking about it, the average Sunderland mentality is a bit like the Scots (or Scotch as they love to be known) and their attitude towards the English. The

Scots really despise everything about the English, shown in their absolute support for anyone playing England at any sport. The sad fools even had Maradona banners at the recent Scotland vs Argentina game, in reference to the *Hand of God* incident in 1986 for God's sake! Sunderland fans are a bit like this – more bothered about Newcastle losing than Sunderland winning. Bob Murray summed it up when he said the Stadium of Light would always have one more seat than Newcastle (I know I have already mentioned this). Nice to see where his priorities were – having an extra seat than us. Frankly I couldn't care how big the SOL is.

In the same way I'm not really bothered what happens in Scotland, other than Celtic winning. The Scottish national team is a side I would normally support to an extent, but in the end I don't really care. It's nice when they lose to minnows in a World Cup game, but I suppose I would feel the same if Brazil lost to Malta. My thoughts on Sunderland are the same – only slightly above apathy. Why the red and whites would be happy to go down, just so they could see us relegated, I have no idea.

Middlesbrough

After Pompey's draw at Newcastle, I feel like hope has been renewed again. If Newcastle and Hull continue to be as bad as Boro then whichever one of us can buy a couple of wins should survive. And then there is Sunderland… of course I would far rather have the points and goal difference of Sunderland or Hull but if we could possibly finish the season on a roll then… everything is still possible. Especially as both of them look so vulnerable at home.

Wednesday 29th April 2009
Song for the day: Iron Maiden – Run To The Hills

Sunderland

First day back at work and a ribbing of the highest order is received for the horror show at the Hawthorns last Saturday – the buggers don't forget do they? More jokes concerning Newcastle are doing the rounds in time to cheer my spirits. I decide to start one on the texts to see how long it will take to turn full circle and reach its way back. It reads…

'There is a new virus doing the rounds. The symptoms are a mixture of Bird and Swine Flu and also thinking Newcastle will stay up. It's called Flying Pig Flu.'

Childish I know, but today work is slow and the office banter passes the time. Hopefully, all of the Everton team will have contracted a mild dose of Swine Flu for Sunday, as then we may have a chance of a home victory.

I had another go at the BBC football predictor table today and even the computer can not work out the final standings come May, it's that tight at the bottom. I have now given up with the predictions game, leaving it all in the hands of fate and what will be will be.

Newcastle United

Apparently today is the anniversary of Kevin Keegan's famous *"I would love it if we beat them, love it!"* speech. Couldn't agree more Kev. I would love it if we stopped up, love it.

All talk at the moment that I come across seems to be simply based on everyone predicting the results of every match and working out where their team will end up. Strangely most Sunderland fans predict they will stay up and we will go down, with most Toon fans thinking the same. There really is a lot of pessimism around the Geordies at the moment.

One red and white I know thinks it's because a generation of Newcastle fans have only known the team from The Entertainers onwards. Most fans under 25 possibly won't remember the 80s shambles we went to watch in the ramshackle old stadium. All they know is Ginola, Shearer, Beardlsey, Robert, Speed etc gracing a plush grassy pitch in the huge, new SJP. Not many have even heard of Frank Pingle, Franz Carr, Rob McDonald, Pat Heard (canny Masters player), Wes Saunders, George Reilly, Tony Cunningham and Malcolm Brown.

Sunderland on the other hand have experienced relegation and promotion battles practically every year. They have regularly seen dross, so know what to expect and how to survive going down. A lot of younger Toon supporters do not.

Middlesbrough

I interviewed Middlesbrough Football Club in the Community chairman George Cooke today. (George was awarded an MBE in the Queen's Birthday Honours List in the summer). George is about to embark on Wainwright's Coast-to-Coast walk, about 196 miles in all. He was in training 3-4 hours a day so that despite having a couple of metal hips he and the community team would be able to complete the walk, although it would not be the stroll in the park that Julia Brad-bury made it look. The aim was to raise money and awareness for Boro summer holiday schemes to be able to "bring kids from the more difficult areas of East Middlesbrough, East Cleveland, Redcar and Stockton onto our holiday courses in the summer."

George told me the community schemes should be OK if we go down. They have got a year's funding from the Premier League, and have managed to secure lots of other funding partners such as the NHS. By developing Astroturf pitches for hire, the hope is that the Community project can be less and less dependent on Premier League funding. In dealing with close to 50,000 people in a year; the community schemes are a massive and extremely important part of Middlesbrough FC's operation. The kudos of the Boro badge can motivate and stimulate where all other avenues struggle or fail. Along with the Academy at Hurworth, the community project is central to Steve Gibson's mission for the club in trying to serve the entire community on Teesside.

George gave me one startling stat that showed the value of their work.

"The principle (of a secondary school in Middlesbrough) said of 200 kids they took in this year at age eleven, 120 in his opinion were obese or over weight. So we went in and did some work and it has been actually quite successful and we are writing up for the health service to show what we can achieve and hopefully they'll fund us to do work in the other secondary schools in Middlesbrough."

Thursday 30th April 2009
Song for the day: Utah Saints – New Gold Dream (81-82-83-84)

Sunderland

Outside the world of football today marks a poignant day. It is the official handover of power in Iraq, from British control to the United States. The handover passes without a flicker at work, as operations are still ongoing in other areas of the Middle East and Afghanistan in particular and it is the current battles that require such attention. In the background though, a memorial service is shown on the BBC for the 179 fallen troops in Iraq, highlighting once more there is more to life than football.

The weekend match versus Everton mirrors last weekend's work format of me being at work the night shift before a game. As the Everton game has been switched for live TV on the Sunday, it allows me to at least catch up on some sleep first, before departing to nearby Wootton Bassett and the Waggon and Horses in particular to take in the game.

It could transpire to be a Super Sunday (for Sunderland at least) as in a quirk of fate that football tends to produce; both bitter North East rivals (the Skunks and us) are playing both Merseyside clubs. Liverpool play the Mags first, followed by the Toffees at the SOL.

Meanwhile back in the far off land of manager Ricky Sbragia, he reckons Everton may have one eye on the looming FA Cup Final with Chelsea. What pills have they been feeding the poor bastard now? I will have some of what he's taking; it will ease the anguish on Sunday.

Sunderland fans are planning revenge attacks on the internet for the Gillingham relegation match back in 1987. As many Sunderland fans will note, during the game between the Gills and the Lads – a relegation play-off (no such thing exists now) which confirmed our demise to the third tier of English football for the first and only time since in our history, several banners and shirts depicting Newcastle were spotted in the away end afterwards and riotous scenes ensued. The slightly bad blood turned into gangrene that day between the two clubs.

Now eyeing up Fulham's away game at St James' Park in two weeks, a large contingent of travelling Mackems aim to infiltrate the Fulham end in the hope that a). Sunderland are safe by then and b). Newcastle are on the brink of certain relegation and that particular match will send them down. The Fulham internet forums have been awash with requests from interested red and white parties wishing on attending and supporting the Londoners for this game. It will be interesting to see how the scenario pans out. The words hell and on spring to mind if it happens.

Newcastle United

Michael Owen has effectively said we will get nothing at Anfield on Saturday, and let's be honest, most of us are thinking of nothing more than damage limitation. Another drubbing like the 5-1 defeat at home will practically wipe out our slightly better goal difference, and could seriously damage the mindset of the team.

Of course Shearer is being upbeat, and saying that we are capable of getting a result. There is always a chance, but being truthful, I will be delighted with a draw, never mind a win.

Middlesbrough

Young full back and former youth team captain Tony McMahon signed a contract today and pledged his future to Boro. Great timing. Let us hope that Tony's example can inspire us to victory on Saturday.

I tried to write a rousing editorial for the Boro v Man United fanzine this morning.

It has been a ridiculously disappointing season. Each glimmer of hope has been followed by the sound of a big door clanking shut. Our appalling away run continues, our terrible luck goes hand in hand with this poor form. I can't believe how many times I have written off Boro's chances only to then tune into TV coverage of an even more hapless display by Newcastle, Hull or Sunderland. They all appear to get worse, which is why you have to think an outrageous result today for Boro and maybe just maybe, no I won't say it!

Man United are well and truly embroiled in a Champions League battle with Arsenal. At 1-0 up, after the first leg, the game is certainly still there to be won. Can we somehow take advantage and find some tiny chink in the armour or concentration of this most professional of clubs? Well, we've done it before. And how often has it been at a similar stage of the season. Please can this yet again be the one game where Man United take their eye off the ball and Boro take advantage, flying at them from the start.

There will be no Carbone, Mendieta or even Brian Deane today, but could Tuncay Sanli be the man? Alongside Tuncay it is great to welcome back the returning hero Didier Digard. Combine them with football swift Gary O'Neill and we will have an engine room of perpetual motion where the mantra will be work, work, work, pass and move, pass and move. Our midfield will punch holes into United defences, especially if they are without Ferdinand and the attack needs to take advantage.

The unexpected return of Digard could have a ripple effect through the side and the supporters. He's going to be a special player, other teams know how influential he is for us; it's not just Lee Cattermole that has kicked him off the park this campaign. There has rarely been a match where Didier hasn't been whacked again and again.

Let's lift the roof today, turn on the hairdryers and let Man United feel the force of Teesside. You never know you could be part of something very special indeed. Come on Boro - one massive effort today. We've done it before, do it again and it will save our lives.

NORTH

EAST

PASSION

I The Diary May 2009

Friday 1st May 2009
Song for the day: White Lies – To Lose My Life

Sunderland

This weekend could play a pivotal role in the outcome of the relegation zone. If Sunderland can somehow manage a positive result (that includes a draw) and Boro and the Mags suffer their predicted defeats against the big boys (Man United and Liverpool respectively) then the Hamlet cigars can come out of the closet. Lest we forget what happened last week in the Ricky (Sbragia) Horror Show and I must eradicate this strain of optimism out of my system before it becomes contagious. Maybe I am suffering the early stages of Swine Flu, which seems destined to make the human race extinct, or so the press would have you believe.

It would surely be no match for the Sunderland Syndrome I have encountered for the past 30 years, in which the patient has an initial reservoir of hope, which empties at a daily rate, eventually lying dormant, never brimming with capacity ever again. I should know better than to have a ray of hope. There was even a Sunderland fanzine entitled. 'It's The Hope I Can't Stand' which simply sums up the angst that fellow sufferers of this disease endure.

Today's programme listings on the box serve as a reminder to the testament that things are never straight forward following the red and white cloth. Casually pottering around the house, flicking through TV channels, I stop at ITV 4 as they play re-runs of ITV's 1970s football show The Big Match. Today's show centred upon the promotion race in April 1979, three months before I was born. Crystal Palace, Brighton and Sunderland were all battling to be in Division One the following season, with Sunderland languishing in third place, with a caretaker manager in charge (sound familiar?) in the form of Billy Elliott.

Third place back then was good enough for promotion – no play offs in those days, yet Sunderland seemed intent on throwing it all away, with ITV showing that day's sorry home defeat to Cardiff City. On a day we could have reached the summit of the league, we mess it up, allowing others to take control and congregate around us.

This was before I was born and it has been the bloody same since. Perhaps we are cursed and the ironic 'lucky' nickname of the Black Cats is doing us no favours. Perhaps we used all our luck as a club on the 5th May 1973, who knows? It certainly feels like it. Just when one thinks we have turned the corner... the Denis Smith era, Peter Reid's tenure, the arrival of Roy Keane and saviour, Niall Quinn, it all turns to rat shit and flows down the swanny.

There is also a flip side to that murky coin. When everything looks bleak and the writing is on the wall, the team either pull it out of the bag against the elite, or some messiah washes up on the shores of Seaburn beach to pull the club out of the doldrums, albeit for a brief period.

The defeat against West Brom last Saturday left us with a mountain to climb, but I would not bet against Sunderland to do it the hard way – probably something stupid like beating Chelsea at home on the final day of the season because no drama on the final day of a season would just be unlike Sunderland. For one, the fans would not know what to do with themselves. Sunderland AFC has to be one of the most exciting clubs to follow, whether it is for the right or wrong reasons, or sometimes downright embarrassing reasons, that's a fact.

Newcastle United

May arrives and signals the final days of football for another season. Championships, promotions, relegations and of course the FA Cup Final in England plus the European finals will all be decided over the next month. I hope we don't finish up in the relegated category and still believe we won't although again we are hoping results tomorrow go our way. I don't expect anything other than bad news from Anfield and with Gerrard returning they will be banking on a comfortable win. Apparently Owen may be dropped against his former club – big decision to make if it's true.

Middlesbrough

I was interviewed for Sky Sports today along with Paddy of the Middlesbrough Disabled Supporters Association and Danny from Twelfth Man. We were standing in front of the stadium trying to find some brave words of inspiration before the Man United match. I was quite bullish – we would be the underdogs, we would go for it and this would be the win that would rescue us from the grip of relegation. I was thinking back to our win over Liverpool in February and also past victories against Man United. Go out there, win it and survive.

Interview with Keeper Ross Turnbull in the lead up to Boro v Man Utd played on Sat May 2nd, from Fly Me To The Moon fanzine.

Fly Me To The Moon: *We're in the final games now and there is a big struggle ahead. What frame of mind are the players in do you think?*

Ross Turnbull: *I think it's a good frame of mind. We know what our capabilities are and we've got some difficult games coming up but we've shown this season in patches that if we play well we could pick up enough points to get out of the situation that we are in.*

Fly: *We can't afford to draw anymore can we? We need to win now don't we?*

RT: *Yes definitely, we've got to set out and go and win games. On Saturday set out to attack Man United and not sit back - try and win the game, I think that's what we will do. And it's just getting a bit of luck and a little break that we haven't had recently.*

Fly: *On Sunday for instance?*

RT: *Yes the penalty decision and the offside for their first goal. That bit of luck that we maybe haven't had all season but I'm sure we might get one between now and the end of the season and hopefully it will go our way.*

Fly: *We've got to capitalise on that.*

RT: *Yes if we do get a decision we've got to take it and it's important that we win matches. So we've got to score goals to do that.*

Fly: *So nobody's thinking about relegation?*

RT: *No we're not. Everyone is just concentrating game by game and I think we all understand the situation that we're in and it's just vitally important that we go out and perform and attack teams and pick up three points whenever we can.*

Saturday 2nd May 2009
Song for the day: Whitey – Non Stop

Sunderland

It is 13.45 and I am awake from last night's shift. Do I wander over to the TV and view the Boro v Man United score, which has kicked off early, or wait for the result, akin to the Likely Lads TV programme, when the characters waited all day without a word of the final score to watch England on the highlights show later that night, only for the match to be postponed without their knowledge.

I will leave the result for later, when I tune in for the remainder of the day's final scores in a show of football masochism, living on the edge, denying myself the pleasure of hearing Boro's latest downfall... for a while at least.

My mate Ant Morton texts me. He is an avid Everton fan and normally tries to take the piss, but he is quite serious about tomorrow's game, stating that he would accept a point in their quest for European football. I inform him that after witnessing that shower of shit last week, I would gladly cartwheel up the M1 and show me tezzas in Jacky White's market, if Sunderland secured a point on Sunday, after all Stephen Hawkins and Stevie Wonder would have had more chance of finding the net than either of Kenwyne Jones or Djibril Cisse.

I make a cup of tea and try somehow to return to the land of nod... it is safer there away from all of this football nonsense.

My football sabbatical is abruptly ended when our lass phones to say Boro are 0-2 down with only minutes to play. It looks as though Fergie's second string are too much for Boro. A rumour is circulating now that the Smoggies are on the verge of administration themselves. I reckon both Boro and the Mags should call in the receivers now, hold up their hands and take the points deduction punishment on the chin and allow the good guys in all this (namely Sunderland) to stay up and take their rightful place in England's elite. No, I can't see that happening either, but one can hope.

It transpires that Blackburn and Portsmouth both suffer heavy defeats at the hands of Manchester City and Arsenal respectively. It appears the two clubs are not out of the mire just yet, with goal difference possibly coming into play. Maybe there is some hope for all three North East sides to stay up. Hull still look doomed with abominable form, whilst the two clubs mentioned here are no world-beaters. It is as if no one wants to stay up, every week twists and turns occur. One minute you are fading away into the Championship, the next we're booking our hotels for next season's assault on Europe.

The opportunity is there for Sunderland to grab with both hands tomorrow and we will be home and dry, all but in mathematics.

Newcastle United

Not a bad day today. Everyone around us managed to get themselves beaten. Boro started it all off by getting beat, rather predictably, off Man Utd 2-0. This was the live lunchtime game so was nice to see the defeat happening. Later on in the day Blackburn, Stoke and Portsmouth all lost as well. While these three aren't the teams we will be aiming to catch, it just about keeps them in the mix and still needing points.

The rumours persist that Shearer will drop Michael Owen, and go with Martins and Viduka, or maybe even a five man midfield.

Middlesbrough

I have been trying to forget today's game all week. Play it cool, don't get forced down by the pressure. Talk of late injuries to Boro team members Taylor and O'Neill is less a priority for me after finding out that first one then two and now three of my fanzine sellers can't make it. Late last night I found an email from Josh that he couldn't attend and I was lucky enough to get a replacement in at midnight. Then just as I pulled into the office, Garry rang to say he couldn't stop being sick, fortunately his friend John said he would come over once he was up! Like I said there were things going on that helped take my mind off the match.

But here it is, the time has arrived, can we do the impossible? Not since the Mc-Claren days have we been United's nemesis – no better time to return to the past. Remember Mendieta, Carbone, players that were truly inspired playing Alex Ferguson's team. Let's hope United have their minds on the Champions League. It is only half time after all. Perhaps they will come here thinking it is like half time entertainment, if so then we must give them a quick shock. It's so sad that they can put out a different team and it will still be stronger than everyone else. Still Jonny Evans isn't any Rio Ferdinand and when you are clutching at straws...

This is what I wrote immediately after the game.

Match Report - Dead Men Walking.
Boro 0 Manchester United 2

We all knew in our heart of hearts that winning this game wasn't really a realistic possibility but the way we were outclassed and outplayed can only lead to one conclusion, we are goners. In fact we've already gone, but whatever we do, we simply must beat Newcastle on the way down.

Boro started quite strongly against Man United, a full house, so plenty of backing, with lots of volume and colour from the stands, apart from the packed Man United end, where the lack of red stood out like a sore thumb. Digard remained on the bench, as did Alves with King as target man and Aliadiere's runner up front. Justin Hoyte came in at left back for the injured Taylor, O'Neill on the right, switching with Downing.

History almost repeated itself as Aliadiere again missed a golden opportunity, put through behind the defence, his shot was once again saved. That save by Ben Foster turned the game as did Almunia's block last week at Arsenal. The precision with which Giggs found the bottom corner after Matty Bates was spun round on the edge of the area suggested he is sponsored by Garmin, rather than the Boro players, a lesson for Jeremie?

Funnily enough a couple of the day's highlights came when two fans hit the crossbar in the halftime entertainment. If only Boro players could have the same accuracy.

We were chasing the game in the second half something that has seemed beyond us all season long, when United doubled the lead after 10 minutes we were pretty much sunk. I think I have blanked this goal out of my memory. It just heralded in half an hour of misery, despite the arrival of Digard (for McMahon) and Alves (for King), Boro couldn't find a way past United's defences. Downing and Tuncay worked and worked, Digard showed the 110% attitude we have been lacking in the engine room, but there was no cohesion and no belief. When Alves did make a couple of darting runs he failed to look up and pick out Emnes and overran the ball. An injury time free kick was blazed high over the bar by the Brazilian and summed up his and maybe our season.

It was such a depressing end to a game when Man United in the end performed a master class and Boro had absolutely no way or means to give them a decent game. This match was crying out for the fighting spirit, experience and above all the leadership of George Boateng. He is like the ravens at the Tower of London, we should have clipped his wings and stopped him from fleeing the nest, and without him we are relegated.

So, start preparing for the Championship. You cannot really come to any other conclusion, we lack the firepower, the spirit and it appears the collective ability to stay up. George tried to help us when he gifted us a goal for Hull, but without him we are doomed. It's a daunting road to Doncaster, Ipswich and Crystal Palace. First we have unfinished business, we must beat the Geordies, then we can grieve.

Sunday 3rd May 2009
Song for the day: The Beatles – Yellow Submarine

Sunderland

All aboard the good ship HMS Sunderland (or rather the Flying Boat Sunderland)... steady as she goes Mr Quinn, as we set sail for the calmer waters of Premiership security... well that is the plan.

I wake up early after a few hours recovery from last night's shift, in order to travel some five miles up the road to Wootton Bassett to visit the nearest pub (well the nearest pub with Sky TV). I have to travel these five miles up yonder, as the two so called pubs in the small village of Lyneham do not show any kind of sports and one even advertises itself as a sports bar – hang your heads in shame, especially with a military base around the corner, ready and waiting to offer custom. I have a good mind to contact the advertising standards agency, as surely this is false advertising! Mind you they do offer a poker games night on a Friday for the yokels and the amenities include a pool table, but I have still seen more life in a tramp's vest.

The sporting day starts well with news that Tony Jeffries, Sunderland's newest sporting celebrity-cum-Olympic medallist boxer, has won his homecoming and first professional fight at the Crowtree Leisure Centre, back home. In front of a partisan sell out crowd, which raised the roof, Jeffries overpowered his German opponent, with Niall Quinn in attendance at ringside. The Quinnmeister would be somewhat ecstatic if that red hot atmosphere could be recreated at the SOL this afternoon against Everton, but then do these prima donnas in red and white stripes deserve it as much as our lad Jeffries, after the diabolical season so far. I suppose we need to all put our differences to one side and join forces, support the team and keep our ship floating.

Reading the News of the World, Quinny has an interview in there stating if Sunderland just merely limp over the line come the end of the season, then this will suffice, as it will be all change in the summer, beyond recognition apparently and for the better. The club would be nowhere near any more relegation battles, he goes on to say and such will be the financial investment and business acumen of owner in the wings, Ellis Short, that Sunderland will once again be a force in the top flight.

Ha'way Lads – just get over that finish line in one piece... if not for Niall's sake, then for yourselves.

Newcastle United

Strange team news with Owen dropped, and also no Fernando Torres for Liverpool. Normally that would be good news about Torres, but firstly it shows the esteem we are held in, and secondly, he didn't play against us at St James' and we still got thumped 5-1. That was the game where you could tell by Shay Given's body language that he had had enough. Sure enough, he was away to the mighty Manchester City soon after.

Liverpool 3 – 0 NUFC

What can you say? Damage was limited after being two goals down within half an hour and therefore our slender goal difference advantage over Hull remains, but they play on Monday. Twenty odd goal attempts by the Reds to around three by us, and to add insult to injury, Joey Barton's return saw him sent off for a bad (but not terrible) tackle on Alonso. Being honest, the tackle was pretty needless as Alonso wasn't going anywhere, but having said that, while it was full blooded and reckless, I don't think it warranted a straight red, a yellow would have sufficed. In fact, Alan Smith performed a worse two-footed tackle earlier, which only received a caution. A case of Barton's reputation going before him? I'm pretty sure if someone like Alonso or Torres made a similar tackle they would not be sent off. Still, Shearer agreed with the red afterwards, so that means the season is over for Joey with a three-match ban. Big Al did not look happy.

Sunderland managed to turn in an inept home performance and lost 0-2 to a very ordinary Everton side. It keeps them right in the danger area. Defensively they look almost as shoddy as us – and that is saying something!

Middlesbrough

Last night I was out at a gig in town at Westgarth Social Club, where there was a bit of ribbing from Peter – onetime singer of the Nivens and long-time Leeds fan. God I hope we aren't playing Leeds United next season. Jon Lymer reckoned that the Championship could be a welcome respite from years of slog and energy-sapping defeats. Someone else supplied an interesting theory; that they hope Newcastle don't go down because they have the resources to win the league and so it would leave less places to fight for. An interesting theory but I can't think that far ahead.

Anyway, here's hoping Newcastle's defence is as poor as usual today at Anfield.

I decide I can't watch the Newcastle vs Liverpool game, probably better to get gripped by the excitement of the last day of the Championship, will we be involved next year I wonder? I might be able to face watching Hull tomorrow, not sure. Either could be a mortal blow for our chances, which already look almost completely washed out. I know, I know I kept saying to myself and anyone else within earshot that the Arsenal and Man United games were not the decisive games, they were opportunities for bonus points; the real points scoring starts now, but I can't help feeling our confidence is drained, players and fans alike. You can't keep kidding yourselves and trying to hit back when the tank looks so empty.

I listened to some of the Liverpool vs Newcastle match whilst driving over to our mam and dad's for Sunday dinner. I better say lunch because my mam might read this and she'll tell me off. It sounded like Newcastle were playing quite well, then Viduka headed a ball back towards his own area and Newcastle couldn't get it clear, a Liverpool goal was soon followed by another and it sounded as if the Newcastle team were unravelling again. I certainly enjoyed my meal.

Afterwards dad was flicking across to Ceefax whilst we watched the Championship endgame being played out. The score line stayed the same 2-0 until after the game should have finished, obviously there is no one working at Ceefax this Bank Holiday weekend. We flicked over to ITV Teletext to find out Liverpool had won 3-0 and better still Joey Barton had been sent off. It was another needless and appallingly reckless tackle, which could have cost Alonso a broken leg, but had now cost Newcastle the services of Joey Barton for the season. Looking at Smith and Butt they definitely needed the assistance of the younger man, someone that could take the play deep into the opponent's box. What a miss Barton would be, suddenly I was feeling slightly more optimistic again.

Then I sat down to watch Sunderland at home to Everton, it was a game that looked destined for 0-0, but the Sunderland players looked tense. A tension that was clearly shared by the supporters who sat in near silence throughout, then a moment's brilliance by man of the match Pienaar unlocked the Sunderland defence and there was surely no way back. When Fellaini added a second from Pienaar's cross it was all too easy.

A thought crossed my mind again that these two teams do not look as if they are going to get a single point more this season. That means IF we can beat Newcastle, we may have a chance after all. 37 points could be enough with Sunderland and Hull not looking capable of winning. As I clamber up the stairs after Match of the Day, a hundred different permutations are passing through my brain. I can see us beating Newcastle and finally ending our woeful away run, then we can move up and push them down at the same time. There is one massive stumbling block however, how are we going to overcome our horrendous goal difference?

Katie, who was recently Boro's rep on Fan Zone, text me and said that she felt Aston Villa held the key to everything with key games against relegation candidates including us. Now for Monday night I suppose, would it be too much to ask not only for a Villa win but a good sound thrashing for Hull?

Monday 4th May 2009 – Bank Holiday
Song for the day: Jimi Hendrix – Who Knows

Sunderland

No comment. Sunderland 0 Everton 2 and I still have not calmed down, going through a realm of emotions since and just like the players… I simply can't be bothered anymore. I feel demoralised and drained, no energy to continue on.

Newcastle United

Drink Holiday Monday. Star Wars Day – May the fourth be with you!

The repercussions of yesterday's defeat continue, as it seems Shearer tore into Barton after the game, informing him basically that he had let everyone down with his dismissal. Barton responded by saying that he is the best player at the club, and Shearer is a shit manager with shit tactics, as well as calling Iain Dowie a prick - allegedly. As you can imagine, Shearer became a bit miffed and I would guess Barton is lucky to still have his head attached.

At least there was a bit of good news as Hull went down 1-0 against Aston Villa, with John Carew scoring the only goal. Hull had a good go and showed lots of fight but couldn't get an equaliser. The league now looks like this.

POS	TEAM	PLAYED	GD	POINTS
11	WIGAN	34	-7	42
12	BOLTON	35	-11	39
13	STOKE	35	-17	39
14	POMPEY	35	-18	38
15	BLACKBURN	35	-20	37
16	MACKEMS	35	-17	35
17	HULL	35	-23	34
18	NEWCASTLE	35	-19	31
19	SMOGGIES	35	-26	31
20	BAGGIES	35	-31	28

Middlesbrough

Aston Villa 1 Hull City 0

Good old George Boateng for helping us out once again, mugged by two Villa players in the build up to the Villa goal, it was certainly nerve racking at the end as Hull piled forward and Villa started to buckle. Villa hadn't won a home game for months and the tension really got to them, but they held on. So the pressure piles on Hull and now that they have finally managed a home win again, Aston Villa can do us further favours there, as the Geordie Barcodes visit the Midlands on the last day. As for Hull an injury to skipper Ian Ashbee looked bad, that could be costly. The way the players were arguing before half time doesn't actually bode well for their ability to cope with the pressures, without their skipper. Suddenly I'm left thinking of "ifs" and "buts" again. It's all about Monday vs Newcastle, it is all about inflicting a knock out blow on the Geordies and hoping no one else can grab a point in the meantime.

Does anyone want to stay in the Premier League this season?

Tuesday 5th May 2009
Song for the day: Coldplay – Glass Of Water

Sunderland

Only now do I dare go near a piece of paper to enable me to record my feelings. Sunday's performance was the mirror image of the previous week's shite at West Bromwich. Even though players and club officials were drivelling to the press stating how sorry they were, how it was totally unacceptable to not even be at the races at the Hawthorns one week, to repeat the act the following game versus Everton (who apparently have one eye on the cup final and were there for the taking) is a complete DISGRACE.

I do not care if we are not good enough in the skill department as long as we have tried, had a go, done our best, given 100 percent and more. This can be justified to the paying public… somewhere along the line. On Sunday though, the tosspots in red and white should have simply played under the cover of bank notes, as this is where their true colours lie…. the colour of money. If Sunderland do go down, the players will not be there to dust down and fight for promotion, they will be away like the true soldiers of fortune that they are.

The manager is no better. Devoid of any tactical inclination, he drops Tainio, Sunderland's better holding/defensive midfielder as a supposed punishment for his display at West Brom, along with Andy Reid and Carlos Edwards. None of the players performed at Albion, but all are capable of redeeming themselves… unlike the shite that is Whitehead and co operating the middle of the park on Sunday.

Perhaps we should start playing the reserves, youth team or even the fucking ladies' team next week at Bolton. All of them are top of their respective leagues and all have at least an ounce of desire in them. Quinn asks for support but until the man in charge (Sbragia) has departed, this will fall on deaf ears.

At the pub in Wootton Bassett (The Waggon and Horses), I bumped into another exiled Rokerite, also enjoying the humiliating 3-0 defeat dished out to the Mags earlier in the day at Liverpool. He offered me a seat in his car for Pompey away in a fortnight, easing my concerns about travel arrangements to the South Coast. After the second dose of humble pie dished out by a Merseyside club to the North East contingent that afternoon, I declined his offer, stating that I would rather lick stamps than watch anymore of that torture in live mode this season. He offered the appraisal of 'at least the Mags got beat too', but this comment reacted with my brain like phosphorus reacts with oxygen, igniting into an argument that his type of attitude is what gets us where we are now, settling for second best, as long as every other fucker in the region are wasting away, then we can too. I left the pub upset and annoyed.

It seems that no one wants to stay up. All clubs afraid to go for the jugular in case they make a costly mistake, however the biggest mistake seems to be the fact no one has the balls to go for glory. There is no glory in standing back and hoping for the best. SHOW SOME BOLLOCKS!

In a weekend where Boro also looked like lambs to the slaughter, the final results read North East 0 North West 7. I have never known the state of the region's football to be so bad. The hotbed of soccer? More like the sickbed.

Newcastle United

The big news today is the continuing Shearer-Barton bust up. The club issued a statement, which simply read; *"Newcastle United can confirm that Joey Barton has been suspended from the Club until further notice. The Club will be making no further comment on the matter at this time."*

Barton will also be fined around £120,000 for his part in events at the weekend. Barton it seems is one of those players who will be pilloried for everything he does. Sure, he has baggage and has blotted his copybook on more than one occasion, but as I have mentioned earlier, would one of those "great professionals" like Ryan Giggs receive the abuse Joey does, if he committed a similar faux pas? The club has also suspended Barton indefinitely, which means he won't even be training with the squad between now and the end of the season. This tends to suggest that if Shearer stays on as boss, Barton will be looking for a club in the summer, with his contract terminated by the club. The £5.8m buy from Man City will not have a problem finding a new club, especially as a free agent. Put your money on one of the newly promoted Midlands clubs, Wolves or Birmingham, to snap him up pre-season.

It has also been revealed that Shearer supposedly had a rant at some of his players last week, saying *"You are not going to take the piss out of this football club, and you are not going to take the piss out of this city."* You tell 'em Al.

The first team in the Champions League Final was decided when Man Utd gave Arsenal a bit of a lesson at The Emirates, winning 3-1 to go with their 1-0 win at Old Trafford.

Middlesbrough

I watched Arsenal's Champions League hopes wrecked by Man United in 11 minutes. Geoff Vickers of Middlesbrough Supporters South sent me a text pondering whether anyone will mention the last English team to be three goals down at home in a European semi final (Boro versus Steaua Bucharest). Of course no one does, we are the forgotten team. It is yet another reminder of just how far we have fallen.

Wednesday 6th May 2009
Song for the day: Fleetwood Mac – Little Lies

Sunderland

Still no news of Sbragia's departure from Sunderland and so I decide to conjure up my own rumour. I email Sky Sports News under a different guise, commenting on Sbragia's imminent departure. Now I need to start the texts and see how far the Chinese rumour can travel. Hopefully all the way to Niall Quinn, who will go along with the masses and fire the beleaguered Scot.

Meanwhile in the real world, loanees Roy O' Donovan and Anthony Stokes return to their full-time employers after temporary deals at Blackpool and Crystal Palace expire, whilst news comes to light that Michael Chopra's loan deal at Cardiff City will be made permanent on July 1st for a fee of 4 million pounds, apparently it was agreed in February. It would be nice if the supporters knew what was going on now and again and I just wonder if this affected Chops' scuffed shot-cum-cross in the Tyne-Wear derby, earlier in February. The next day he was away to South Wales.

Away from Sunderland, Manchester United were awesome last night in the Champions League Semi Final with Arsenal. However the sending off of Darren Fletcher is simply appalling and is so typical of the modern game, now ruined by the idiots in charge at FIFA. He was accused of 'denying a goal scoring opportunity' because in the end he got the fucking ball! Apparently there is no appeal process to rescind his red card punishment, what utter bollocks… honour fair play? It is about time FIFA start applying their principles to themselves. In any other walk of life there would be an appeal process, be it shop floor union reps, an appeal committee or an appeal process. Surely that stands against the whole spiel of human rights verbal diarrhoea we get spouted by freedom groups when daring to eject illegal foreign citizens and the fact we give them all a fair trial.

Ha ha, I have received two responses from the texts I have beamed around the world, informing everyone that the Sunderland gaffer has left. Both are excited which in effect tells its own story. I've done my bit on Facebook with regards to my status… 'Mal Robinson hopes the rumours that Sbragia have left the club are true, especially if the rumour that training has been cancelled is true'. I might email everyone else connected with SAFC now. I'll get my spoon out and start stirring this mentholated concoction of evil rumour brew.

Ha, the seed is planted, the bandwagon is rolling. I have taken advantage of the fact training has been cancelled, or rather moved to the SOL for the day. People are confirming that indeed the training has been cancelled on the net, thus confirming my initial planted seed of doubt and the rumour is born. It will spread quicker than Swine Flu.

The rumour has reached Setanta via a mate who has called them personally. Rather unsurprisingly they have denied all knowledge of it. The Sunderland press office has also been telephoned by another associate. I now feel a little guilty, but I still have a little giggle about it all.

The rumour is dying earlier than anticipated; now officially on its feet. Training was held behind closed doors at the SOL as confirmed by many on the internet, quashing the suspicious nature of why training was cancelled.

Still at least I got the bastards at SAFC working for a change, even if I got a few hopes raised – sorry lads. It just goes to show how many wanted Sbragia out. It's a pity Quinny cannot see it. If the interview Quinn gave in the News of the World was true about Sunderland surviving and the transformation of the club will be unrecognisable come the summer, leading to a 100 per cent progression both on and off field, why oh why would you risk it all on a 100-1 random outside chance in Ricky Sbragia. He simply could not inspire Lemmings to jump off a cliff. I just cannot fathom football and SAFC in particular out sometimes.

I thought the rumour mill was dead and buried, but more and more people keep writing... 'Hoping Sbragia's gone' on their Facebook status. I feel like the little boy who cried Ricky Sbragia – ha ha. I will probably get lynched now for starting the fucker.

I have just heard a nasty rumour to combat my own, possibly outdoing it in its own right. If Sunderland stay up, or go down, either way, Ricky Spag Bol will be in charge next season. If this is the case, then I'm afraid my time spent watching this shower of shite will come to a sabbatical end. I will go and watch local sides – Chippenham Town, Swindon or even Wootton Bassett Town FC. At least they have more drive and ambition. It looks like Niall's magic carpet ride will have been shut down all together, if true.

After trying to cope with the trauma of this latest potential fatal footballing set-back, there is a magpie in my garden. Is this an omen? I will have to go and buy an air rifle now, I can't be having that flying around and pestering my senses.

I thought my 'Sbragia out' rumour had ran its course, when the first instalment of my work has finally hit the message boards on the Ready To Go fans' website. Some lad had posted that his dad received a text this morning at work, reading the same initial message that I slyly produced. I do wonder if that was a cut and paste of the same text I sent to all and sundry? The experiment is a complete success!

Newcastle United

The papers again are full of Joey Barton and what will happen to him. Apparently even by making a loss of £5.8m on his transfer, getting rid of him would save another £7.5m in wages, that's if you believe the red tops any way. Also, Alan Shearer's crack down on the discipline is discussed. According to the media, training was something of an optional extra at the club and Shearer has clamped down, fining players £20,000 for being late the first time, £40,000 the second time and so on. Christ – I'd be dead on time to earn £40,000 a year, never mind to save it from coming off a week's wages!

There has also been talk that the players must all now stay and have lunch together, rather than just heading straight off to the golf course, hairdressers, tanning salon, Merc showroom or wherever they go to spend their afternoons.

Finally, all injured players must stay with the club doctors until 4pm (the poor darlings!). I expect a few of these overpaid clowns don't like this, but on the wages they earn, they should be in attendance all day every day!

UEFA's anti-England agenda showed itself in full force in tonight's second semi final in the Champions League. Chelsea were so blatantly cheated out of the game it's almost laughable. Platini, Blatter and cronies so couldn't stand the thought of another all-England final, that they brought in a ref from Norway, whose previous biggest game was probably Goblingberg against Oslo Rovers, or something like that. He was either a wrong un, or completely bottled it, waving away three or four good penalty claims from Chelsea before Barcelona progressed through with an injury time away goal. The champagne must have been flowing at UEFA! Generally I can't stand Manchester United, but just this once I hope they stick it right up Barca and bring the trophy back to England.

Middlesbrough

I was interviewed over the phone today by features writer Barbara Argument from the Evening Gazette about the Newcastle match. It's no longer just a story for the back pages, there is no doubt about it, and this is a massive game. I'm starting to feel distinctly nervous about it now.

Southgate was misquoted as saying we can't afford to stay up. He doesn't say that at all but points to how much of a struggle financially it is for us now. Boro fans are not too impressed. For me it is a bad sign for the future of the Premier League that it is becoming the domain of the super rich.

Thursday 7th May 2009
Song for the day: Moby - Bodyrock

Newcastle United

Nice to see it's not Newcastle all over the papers today, well, no more than usual anyway. Chelsea and Drogba, the man who beat us in the UEFA Cup Semi Final when at Marseille, dominate the headlines.

Shearer is saying that the weekend's game (well, Monday's anyway) is the biggest game of his career. This is some statement, but he could be right. The cost, in monetary and football terms, of going down is huge - ask Leeds.

Middlesbrough

I was interviewed today by Owen Gibson of the Guardian, he would be writing a feature on the full economic impact and implications of relegation for the three North East centres. He has travelled up to the region and is visiting all three clubs. The whole world obviously knows how serious this game is, up here.

I tell him how it reminds me of the mid-80s, when Boro nose-dived from relegation into liquidation. We suffered recession then, the shipyards closed down, unemployment was up and money was in short supply. The decline of the football club affected everyone's confidence and pride. One thing that stood out for me back in 1986 was the closure of Woolworths in the town centre. I remember thinking of it as a symbol that the town was in trouble. History has repeated itself this season with Woolworths.

Friday 8th May 2009

Song for the day: Foals – Olympic Airways

Sunderland

I am strangely calm about the impending game tomorrow, away at Bolton Wanderers. The two crushing defeats to West Brom and Everton have sapped my soul of enthusiasm and determination to back my team to the hilt. I still harbour ambitions of a 0-1 victory at the Reebok and I play this out in my head whilst daydreaming. A last minute winner from a corner, as the ball bobbles around the six yard box, it somehow ends up at the feet of on-loan centre half Calum Davenport – why on earth is he up there at this late stage of the game – he miskicks the ball, looping it over the home keeper and it spins across the line, sending the 5,000 travelling hordes in red and white into ecstasy. I even clench my fist in exhilaration, in acknowledgement of the potential delight this would administer to fellow fans, believing in my mind for one delayed moment out of the confines of routine life that this cinematic moment actually happened. I think I am going nuts through the stress of it all. No wonder I have grey hair before my time, at the ripe old age of 29. It was not the copious amounts of recreational abuse I've thrown at my body over the years and it's not through a hectic lifestyle, it is all through bloody supporting Sunderland AFC for nigh on three decades. One day the club may be forced to close its doors for business, with the government citing health and safety to the fans as the significant reason behind the enforced closure. SAFC one day to be mothballed for damage to modern society? Stranger things have happened.

My daydream deflects away from the fact that 5,000 ardent fans have sold out our allocation for tomorrow's game. Are they stupid, gullible, insanely loyal? Perhaps. Personally I have had a gut's full of the players' pathetic performances and the manager's apathy after every negative result, at which there have been plenty. He appears to have no self-pride, plenty of pity and not a clue on how to turn things around. I am not being fickle. I have had enough of the let downs and accepting second, sometimes even third best, when I give my all in return.

Sunderland has some of the most passionate fans in the business and for years the club has continued to ignore this and been unable to take advantage of it properly. In a season where the club potentially has the one of the best squads on paper it has ever possessed, we still continue to flirt with relegation. This is the main contributing factor to everyone's bewilderment and annoyance. Why on earth is this happening? I do not understand how someone with no football managerial experience was allowed to take over full time when Roy Keane left the club.

I sit here months after the event (Sbragia's appointment) and still I am left gob smacked, still and silent, not quite comprehending the gross mistake in making this man the gaffer. Even if we stay up, I feel I will be sitting in the sun wondering just how we got away with that one.

Only time will tell if Quinny has a master plan in place up his very long sleeve.

- **Note to self:** Cheer up son, or you will end up in the Priory, enjoying rehab for depression.

Newcastle United

Some goods news for the region today as Gateshead, currently managed by former Toon player Ian Bogie, won their player-off final against Telford at the International Stadium to gain promotion to the Conference, or whatever it's called these days. I remember seeing Bogie in the 80s playing alongside Paul Gascoigne and the lads from the 1985 FA Youth Cup-winning side. He always looked a good player, but never seemed to quite fulfil his promise at Newcastle, though did go on to do quite well in the lower leagues with Preston, Port Vale and a few others.

I actually played for Gateshead for a while at the end of the 80s, when Middlesbrough's current youth team boss, Dave Parnaby, was in charge, so it's nice to see them doing well again after a few years in the doldrums.

Middlesbrough

Total perspective time – Corus the steelworks looks likely to close in Redcar. My mate Kay who I'm attending the Newcastle game with is one of over 2,000 who stand to lose their jobs. It could be absolutely devastating for the whole of Teesside when you think of how many other businesses and workers are dependent on the steelworks. These are terrible times.

Saturday 9th May 2009

Song for the day: La Roux – In For The Kill (Skream's Let's Get Ravey Remix)

Sunderland

It is my sister Anita's birthday today. According to her birth certificate she is 37 years old – ouch! In footballing circles though she is 43 years old. It was three years ago when I wrote to Luton Town Football Club trying to acquire a ticket for Sunderland's last game of the Championship winning season, as the Hatters had only given SAFC around 1,500 tickets or so. Entrance to Kenilworth Road was as tricky as obtaining a ticket for the parting of the seas.

I wrote stating it was Anita's birthday (her 40th) on the day of the game and being a lifelong Luton fan could we get any tickets? An email was returned saying they'd gladly oblige, leading my other sister Helen (who possessed a Southern accent) to coax the club secretary along in order to confirm the purchase of our prized assets. Hence, Anita now has a normal birthday and a football birthday – albeit some six years difference.

All of this effort to see the lads clinch the second tier title and now it could be all thrown away, through lack of passion from the players. Football never stands still. Anyhow, it is match day today and the slightest glimmer of hope dwindles away somewhere deep inside… probably my bowels.

I have already decided not to attend any more games this season, however being honest, travelling to Bolton was always going to be a long shot anyway, with the Reebok being probably one of the hardest places to attend from deepest Wiltshire. And so it will be *Soccer Saturday* for me today. On second thoughts, no. I will have a day of quietness and calm, only glancing to check on the final scores. It will cause less anxiety that way, that is if I am able to stick to my guns.

I am safe in the knowledge that I won't be ridiculed at work for at least a week. Derek in the office supports Bolton and with neither of us daring to mock each other before the game, we both anticipate a much harsher form of piss taking after the final whistle. I know full well, Del Boy will be on the phone, or ready to pounce the following Friday (when he's back in), the sneaky bastard. For this alone, I pray we don't receive an arse whipping today. Ha'way Sun'lun!

Bolton Wanderers 0 Sunderland 0

I tried in vain to stay away from the television set. I go to bed, resplendent in my red and white colours. The deeper I try to go under the duvet covers, the further away from all the pain I try to go. This was the intention anyway. I forget to turn the phone off and of course sod's law decrees that the bugger will ring as soon as I nod off. Seconds out in the land of zeds and brother-in-law Al is on the end of the line, ringing from the pub back home, where he is watching the match via a dodgy satellite channel. I decline the call, and then switch the phone off altogether.

The home phone goes. Do I answer, will it be important? Not important enough that I may hear the football scores by accident. It is duly ignored and off I trot once more to the land of make believe.

It is at this stage, that our lass returns home from work to ask … 'if I know the score?'.

I realise by now that I will not be allowed to rest on my lonesome for a while. To compound things, she goes downstairs and switches on Soccer Saturday. The TV volume is audible just enough to make out the panel of pundits, offering their excitable views, but not loud enough to hear what exactly is making them excited. It is enough though to create butterflies and tension in my stomach. For ten minutes or so I go through the motions of consoling my inner soul that relegation is part and parcel of being a Sunderland fan. We would regroup next season as we always do and launch another promotion bid and no doubt win the league, or come somewhere close. There will be new grounds to visit and more clubs close to my Wiltshire vicinity. With these thoughts in mind, I prepare myself to wander downstairs.

As I gradually move closer to the living room, step by step, the tones from the TV set become clearer, as if I were deciphering a World War II enigma code. I make out West Brom are in the ascendancy against Wigan at the Hawthorns. I walk in to watch Jeff Stelling note … 'and we'll go straight back to the Reebok and Paul Merson.'

Time stands still; I am rooted to the floor, like I have just heard a burglar rummaging through my house.

'Still goalless Jeff', came the reassuring noises from the cockney pundit. I took in a deep reflective sigh, until I noticed the remainder of the game had a good fifteen minutes to play out. From that point on, I mustn't have stayed still for more than five seconds in one place.

Eventually the final whistle blew to earn a valuable point for a Sunderland side completely dominant in the first half, pegged back a little in the second by a resurgent Wanderers side, yet still seemingly fighting for one another, fighting for the red and white cause. This is all we ask as fans.

Hungarian keeper Marton Fulop has been dubbed as producing the fifty million pound save for Sunderland right at the death, keeping us afloat with a fine piece of athleticism, scrambling across his goal to parry away a drifting Bolton header. Paul Merson was orgasmic in his comments afterwards about Fulop's one-handed masterpiece.

West Brom move level on points with Boro and the Mags, with talk of a great escape on the cards. I very much doubt it with the arrival of Liverpool next week for the Baggies. Stoke as it transpires pulled out a massive favour for Sunderland with a 1-2 victory over Hull at the KC Stadium. Blackburn however beat Portsmouth 2-0 at Ewood Park, meaning they are virtually safe… unlike Pompey.

It now boils down to Monday's game between our two local rivals. The winner takes all… well almost. That winner could still be Sunderland, with a nice 0-0 draw on the cards. I visit the BBC Football Predictor once more; I work out my calculations to see if it is still possible for all three North East sides to avoid the drop, even with a draw on Monday at Sid James' Park. The computer says yes for a change, although a minor miracle will be needed.

I go to work this night shift a slightly happier bunny. I would have accepted 0-0 at the Reebok before kick off… now for Pompey next Monday evening.

Newcastle United

What the hell is going on at The Hawthorns? Not content with beating the Mackems (an admirable piece of work), they have now gone and beaten Wigan, and look as if they don't realise they are going down! How dare they! They have actually now drawn level with us and the Smogs on 31 points. It was bad enough worrying about the teams above us moving away, but now we have to look over our shoulder at the ones below us. It's just not cricket!

On the plus side, Stoke did us a massive favour and beat Hull away, pretty much securing their safety, and keeping the Tigers within touching distance of us. The Mackems gained an unlikely point with a drab encounter at Bolton, though Kieran Richardson looked liked he'd been taking shooting lessons from Oba Martins!

This all means that we are still three points behind Hull with a better goal difference, so victory on Monday should lift us out of the bottom three.

Middlesbrough

I'm not very good at listening to football games over the radio. Well, not when they really matter. I've never been able to listen to a full Boro commentary since January 1976. Boro took a 1-0 lead in the League Cup semi-final in the away leg at Manchester City and everyone was Wembley dreaming. We were going to a cup final at last, even Don Revie and Cloughie backed us to do it. In the event we were torn apart from the kick off. The game was a complete catastrophe, hammered 4-0 and never again have I been able listen to the words without pictures to a Boro game.

So, even though Boro weren't playing it was still too important to follow radio commentatory. I went to work instead, editing my website and allowed myself peeks from time to time on the message board as reports filtered in of latest scores. Sunderland held 0-0 at Bolton could have been better, but could have been a lot worse. I had been tipping them to get no more points, well they've got one more but seriously that is probably it for them, safety assured.

It was then over to Hull versus Stoke City, the game that some Boro fans had long picked out as being our final downfall. I wasn't too sure for me, as the teams play similar football, but Stoke have more weapons and a greater confidence. Fortunately they still need points to be absolutely sure, what delight then to hear them taking the lead and then another sneaky look revealed they were 2-0 up. Get in. My nerves could have done without the late rally, however the damage was done. A door was opened on Monday. Over to us now, time to produce for ourselves. Come on Boro!

Sunday 10th May 2009
Song for the day: Artic Monkeys – A Certain Romance

Newcastle United

Again our lower leagues friends did us proud today, with Whitley Bay beating Glossop North End 2-0 at Wembley to lift the FA Vase. Over 12,000 supporters were there to see the match on a beautiful sunny day. There were a couple of former Toon players in the side, but neither had made the first team. So the Heed and the Baysiders win - just need the Toon to do the same tomorrow.

Middlesbrough

I'm thinking well ahead now and would have welcomed a win for Manchester City over Manchester United. My reason being that Hull's final game is at home to United. A defeat for United could take the Premier League title race into the last fixture in which case they will surely hammer Hull City.

Monday 11th May 2009

Song for the day: Pendulum – Hold Your Colour

Sunderland

I was in a relative state of calm. The weekend had petered out in relaxed spirits, everything wasn't exactly rosy, but acceptable none the less. This mood was translated into today and lasted all day until our lass happened to turn on the TV, to reveal Sky Sports News and the hype surrounding the '100 million pound match' began.

With David Craig loitering with intent outside Castle Grey Skull and the usual Geordie suspects hanging off his microphone, Sky Sports News transformed into NUFC TV, forgetting that the Smoggies were also playing in this game and this type of hype is something which boils the piss of most non-Geordies in the region. A stereotypical image of the North East sees pictures of the beaming Angel of the North or Tyne Bridge, with Newcastle being the centre point of the universe for all things Northern. If Geordies made films, they'd have Aliens blowing the shit out of the Baltic Flour Mill and Will Smith flying fighter jets over the skyline of the Blinking Eye bridge, as Newcastle being the most important part of planet Earth, any attack from little green men would surely be focussed on this 'epicentre of self importance.

By the same token, when TV cameras are dispatched to Wearside and Teeside, the media must piss themselves in a sweepstake of how many jobless chav tramps they can interview with no teeth, making a mockery of the area. The likes of the rat boy who lived on the Byker Wall, The Dunston Rocket and Spuggy – the minger from Byker Grove are all forgotten, when posh out of towners from Morpeth and Ponteland are hand picked for interview, outside the entrance to Eldon Square (paid for by the North East citizens' taxes, as is Newcastle Airport) spouting how beside themselves they will be, should the Mags go down. All of this forgotten as is Sunderland, the region's biggest city, perhaps not city centre, but in terms of geographical boundaries – the North East's biggest city. Stick that in your pipe and smoke it, sports reporters.

Unfortunately though I see a home victory, as Boro are even worse than the Mags and just in time to give the media a ceremonial hard on, Michael Owen, everyone's supposed favourite striker will probably score to round off the script.

Everything is about United, Newcastle this, Newcastle that – bollocks to it. I have lost my loaf and this is one of the reasons why I won't buy Sky. They follow predictable football, always churning out the usual shite punditry… 'Newcastle have winnable games…'. Do Boro, Sunderland and Hull not have winnable games? What is a winnable game? Surely anyone participating in a game of football at any level in the world, against any team in the world, has a chance of winning that game, as it is a 90 minute session of competitive sport and so in theory every team looking to compete in a game of football, must be focussed on winning that game, therefore EVERY game is a fucking winnable game. Change the record please. Soon they will be saying 'the next goal will be crucial in this game' halfway through a match…. oops too late!

Glad that's off my chest!

It is full time and apparently Newcastle United have won the league… hang on a minute, I thought so, they have only beaten Boro – a side looking doomed – 3-1, yet one would think the bastards had won the Fairs Cup again. Have they forgotten they have two more games to play yet and all is not over? I mean enjoy the victory, but please keep it in check until the final day of the campaign.

Newcastle United

Big game today. Martins is suffering from a groin strain again, so is on the bench, with Owen recalled alongside Viduka. Collocini is dropped for Steve Taylor and Nolan comes in for the suspended Barton. Guthrie is in the team too with Duff at left back for god's sake. There is still no real creativity in midfield, although Jonas does run around a lot.

NUFC 3 – 1 Middlesbrough

We made hard work of it in the end, but the Tyne – Tees derby finished with three goals in the net, three points in the bag, and hopefully the bottom three a thing of the past, three years since Shearer's Testimonial.

But after three minutes it didn't look quite so good, as we wasted two opportunities, (Viduka nearly snapping a post) and Boro's first attack ended up with Habib Beye trundling the ball into his own net. We were level soon after though, as Steven Taylor powered a header in from Guthrie's corner. Boro are the worst team I have seen all season, and it was in my thoughts that if we couldn't beat them, then we deserve to be relegated.

Owen was subbed in the second half for Martins, who managed to score within a minute of coming on, slipping as he shot but doing enough to put us in the lead. Another sub, Lovenkrands, finished the game off in the last five minutes, to calm the nerves and lift us above Hull on goal difference.

The atmosphere was rousing, with thousands of flags given to supporters before the game, and it was good to see them waving in triumph at the full time whistle. This was the first time in fourteen months we had gone behind and came back to win. Also, this was only our fifth home league win of the season, not good, but the table looks better and I really can't see Hull climbing above us again. (Famous last words?).

POS	TEAM	PLAYED	GD	POINTS
11	WIGAN	35	-9	42
12	STOKE	36	-16	42
13	BOLTON	36	-11	40
14	BLACKBURN	36	-18	40
15	POMPEY	36	-20	38
16	MACKEMS	36	-17	36
17	NEWCASTLE	36	-17	34
18	HULL	36	-24	34
19	SMOGGIES	36	-28	31
20	BAGGIES	36	-29	31

Middlesbrough

Newcastle away. Date with destiny. Very very nervous. There are amazing rumours about the team selection on the fmttmboro message board, all confirmed on BBC Tees. For this our most important game of the season we are playing Shawky in midfield for only his third start this year. Where is Digard? Injured again it seems and probably out for the season. Sickener.... Upfront Marvin Emnes has been given his Boro debut, what a gamble!

Match Reaction

It was an incredible atmosphere at St. James', looking down from our balcony in the sky at all those waving flags and that deafening noise, it was lumps in the throat time. I hoped our players would feel inspired rather than racked by nerves. It was now or never. Win tonight and it means survival, lose and that's it - pack your bags for Plymouth.

This is what I wrote on my website after one of the most devastating defeats I've ever witnessed. Kay and I didn't actually speak from leaving the ground until we were almost back at Teesside, both absolutely gutted!!

Newcastle Utd 3-1 Boro

I can't write a match report tonight. What happened is going to take a long long time to sink in. But for the time being there is numbness, to go one goal up and then for that to happen…

I'm sorry I am a fan not a reporter. Sometimes you are too gutted to write anything. Sleep on it perhaps, but it won't look any better in the morning will it? It's a pity the season couldn't end tomorrow, effectively it did tonight. What a place to be sent down, at St. James' Park with all their black and white flags, with all their Shearer worship. It's the end of the road for our Premier journey. It's a hard thing to take, in many ways it's going to get harder still. It will take a long, long time to eradicate the nightmares from tonight's crushing experience at Newcastle.

Not much more to be said tonight. The end of a dream…

Simply devastating.

Tuesday 12th May 2009
Song for the day: Kaiser Chiefs – Everything is Average Nowadays

Newcastle United

The air of gloom is now lifted and everyone is optimistic about Newcastle and Sunderland staying up (sorry Boro – you're doomed), so the good-natured banter at work has pretty much dried and now the topic of conversation is more about how the *'hotbed of football'* can produce three such awful teams. Being honest, you don't really feel as if you could put a good side out with all three squads at your disposal!

Middlesbrough

I started writing about the match again this morning.

Boro's Premier bubble finally burst at St. James' Park last night. The door to safety opened over the weekend and was slammed shut in sickening fashion. What could be worse than being "effectively" relegated at Newcastle? Horrible.

It will take some getting over last night. It is still hard to put it into words…

I've got to be honest I am so fed up and thoroughly sickened that I don't want to continue this diary any further. We're going down now and I would rather not have Newcastle and Sunderland fans mocking me and my words. I'll contact the fellas to tell them I cannot write anymore now. Like my team I'm down and out now.

(I wrote the following piece for Saturday's fanzine versus Aston Villa. One of the gloomiest, most pessimistic doom-laden fanzine's I've ever been associated with)

Where Did It All Go Wrong?

It all seems so long ago now, the promise at the start of the season or even before that when we were flying last summer. We could not stop scoring goals. The exciting attacking football Gareth Southgate had long promised seemed about to be delivered. Afonso Alves looked like he was going to smash goalscoring records, some astute tipsters even had him down to take the golden boot. Yes the season started with a real buzz, it was like going back to 96/97. Oh dear.

It is not with hindsight that I invoke comparisons with our last relegation season. There was a genuine buzz around the town; a new spirit at the club and with imaginative ticketing initiatives there was a whole new generation coming into the Riverside. And much like 96/97 the season started with so much promise and victories. Even our defeats were unlucky and Gareth Southgate deservedly won the manager of the month award. Amazing to think about that now from the ruins of relegation.

But from the onset there were also the danger signs of 96/97. In pre-season I was interested to watch how the young, inexperienced side handled setbacks. I made a mental note that we must be patient and take the long view, it was a bold move for youth and it could go wrong before it went right. As it happens the gamble on inex-

perience was too great. Alves failed comprehensively to get anywhere near the goal form of the end of last season never mind fulfil the £12m goal machine tag. Players that were thought of as pivotal midfielders like Arca and Shawky just couldn't cut it. It's hard not to conclude that we sold and released the wrong midfielders.

I understood why we cleared out the engine room. Basically we were too slow and paid the penalty with booking after booking and suspension after suspension. But personally I would have retained Boateng and probably Rochembeck as well. I thought and said at the time that we should have built up and around an experienced midfield. Digard was bought for the future, Gareth Southgate said so at his signing, so what about the present?

I spoke with Southgate at the Digard/Emnes press conference and asked him about George Boateng who was talking with Hull on that very day. Gareth acknowledged the incredible performances of George after the Cardiff disaster in the Cup Quarter Finals and how pivotal his role was in galvanising the team and stopping what could have been a crash dive to relegation. But he said he was "comfortable" with him leaving, it was George's decision to make. I could understand that we couldn't afford to guarantee him a first team place and that he hadn't cut it as captain but still thought it a big risk. We've lacked leaders on the field ever since Southgate has been in charge. Was Boateng's failure to take to captaincy the start of our slide or was it our failure to replace him? The Cattermole situation disappoints me, his indiscipline off the field is legendary and I believe did impact and impinge on his playing. But our failure to get to grips with young players like that is a weakness that we cannot afford.

So where to now? Well, we must make absolutely certain we are in pole position to bounce back immediately; we must be closer to a Reading or Birmingham than a Charlton. That means the club must make difficult decisions. In the same way that Chief of Operations, Neal Bausor, carried out a root and branch investigation and surgery to the commercial arm of the club we need to leave no stone unturned in stripping away the inadequacies of the playing side of the club. Bausor decided that some senior figures had to go and has carried out a mini revolution at the Riverside, bringing it into the 21st century. We now need an independent troubleshooter to look at the rest of the set-up with the authority to impose equally drastic changes. We need a revolution or evolution at Hurworth as well as the Riverside.

The Academy remains a great success but everything and everyone between our school of excellence and Steve Gibson must be looked at and judged. Things have gone badly wrong. Who and what are to blame? This is not about making scapegoats but more about making sure the club can bounce back and bounce back quickly.

I heard a story mid-season about how Boro had to play two cup games on the same day, it seems no one had realised until too late. We ended up splitting the young squad and bringing in schoolboys for a reserves cup tie at Grimsby. Both games were lost. Someone somewhere had forgotten to switch one of the games. Was this an isolated incident or did it show systemic failure with people not communicating at the club?

There is little doubt that the club had to make drastic savings and so whittled down the squad to a dangerous extent. Senior players on large wage packets were seen as expendable but you literally cannot buy the experience George Boateng, Luke Young and Mark Schwarzer bring to the side. The loss of Young immediately before the season could have been critical to our woefully poor defence. Why did we need the money at that late stage? It obviously wasn't to buy more players.

Some of the trouble has been bad luck. Refereeing decisions in the first part of the season accounted for many dropped points. But most has been self-inflicted. Terrible defending from set pieces continued unchecked, no matter which combination of players were fielded together. No doubt inexperience at the back played a big part but also fingers have to pointed at the coaching. It is unavoidable.

For me the last second miss by Alves against Portsmouth was the single most crucial moment of the season. It was one of the seminal moments when you could sense the true importance right away. I went home and had nightmares about it all night long. I'm not blaming Southgate or Gibson or whoever it was that bought Alves because he came with an incredible track record and remember so many of his goals were set-pieces. Surely with the right technique you can score a free kick at any level. I can barely think of any Premier team that hasn't bought at least one expensive striker who has totally flopped. But it brings us back to 96/97 again when we put too many eggs in one basket. This season we had Tuncay, Downing and Alves - then we had Ravenelli, Juninho and Emerson. There was simply not enough quality back up.

There is so much more to say and so much more to debate on tactics, team selections, substitutions and the like. There were definitely many many mistakes on the part by the manager and his team, but that debate will run on and on through the summer. We could fill this whole fanzine.

So it is with a very sad heart we go into these last two Premier games. You wonder when we will be back here again. I believe it will be a lot quicker if we act smartly now. The club has to open its doors for an inquiry to first learn what has gone wrong and then put the right people and processes in place to come back stronger. No player, coach, manager or executive should be beyond scrutiny. I'm not looking for scapegoats I am looking for a return to Premier League football.

Wednesday 13th May 2009
Song for the day: Rod Stewart – Young Turks

Sunderland

I still haven't looked at the league table since the Mags got lucky against Boro. I have taken a step back from football for a few days mainly for the good of my health. I visited the doctors the other day, only to reveal my blood pressure was higher than usual and I was again suffering from signs of stress. I did not have the heart to tell her I supported Sunderland AFC.

Meanwhile, news that Djibril Cisse will not be here come the start of next season is circling in the papers. Spurs are the club his agent is slipping into conversation in the tabloids. It is of course entirely rumour, but does the club no good, nor help our cause at the moment.

Tonight Wigan play Man United – a game that could have a major influence on the relegation battle. If United win, they only require one point on Saturday against Arsenal at Old Trafford, in order to clinch the Premiership title. Bearing in mind the Red Devils play Hull City away in the last game of the league season and a Champions League final in the offing versus Barcelona only days later and you can only predict a youthful looking United side at the KC Stadium - thus allowing Hull a greater chance of obtaining three vital points, with the permutations most complex and desperate at this stage of the season.

Wigan Athletic 1 Manchester United 2

Michael Carrick scores the winner with four minutes remaining, which could potentially send either us or the Mags down, how ironic being a North East lad as well.

Newcastle United

Today, Crooner Bob at work (staunch Mackem) said he had heard a whisper from a friend who is something to do with Newcastle, that Shearer is about to sign a five year deal with the club. Sounds pretty positive and from the club's point of view, Shearer would probably be given more time to get things right than some other managers. This allows the club to gain a bit of stability and build well instead of building quickly and wrong. Of course this should be applied to any manager, not just a Shearer figure. Stability is something the club has missed in recent years, discounting Keegan the first time round and Sir Bobby Robson's tenure.

Middlesbrough

I was invited on a BBC Tees fans' panel with Alastair Brownlee tonight. Andy Morgan of comeonboro.com website and Paul Welsh, a Boro fan from County Durham, were the other guests. I had not met Paul before and in fact he had never been a guest before but the way he spoke completely changed my mood. Paul argued that a win against Villa would totally alter our outlook. Yes Newcastle might also win but would they follow this up on the road at the same Villa? He thought it unlikely but more to the point how would Hull City and Sunderland cope with the pressures? Hull were away to Bolton, a difficult game. Sunderland had the trickiest task of all away to Pompey but playing after everyone else on Monday. Win against Villa and Sunderland would suddenly be under all kinds of tension, knowing that their final game against Chelsea was almost a write off.

Paul was right. We could yet escape with one good result against a team that had run out of legs and were crawling for their final finishing line, would the players also believe?

I had been invited to buy a ticket for the Middlesbrough Official Supporters' Club player of the season awards afterwards. I decided to opt out. I'm busy finishing this doom-laden fanzine and to be honest am not sure I want to see the players again this season. Near enough the entire first team squad and management are expected to turn out but my disappointment is such that I'd rather not attend.

Thursday 14th May 2009

Song for the day: The Prodigy – Everybody In The Place (Fairground Remix)

Newcastle United

Manchester United grabbed a late winner against Wigan last night, which means they need only a point from the last two games to clinch the title. They have Arsenal at home on Saturday and I'm sure they would love to get the title by beating the Gunners. Really we needed them to drop points last night, or at the weekend so they still need to get something on the last day at Hull, and so hopefully doom them as well as complete their own title charge.

The new shirt was launched today and contrary to the beliefs of my humorous Mackem buddies, I don't think it will be adorned with the Coca-Cola label, not for another twelve months anyway! I also don't expect they were queuing half way down the street waiting for the club shop to open, as has been the case in previous seasons.

Middlesbrough

Just finishing the fanzine and the fans that have written the articles are not a happy bunch. Depression and anger abounds. Skeelo writes "it looks like the shit has hit the fan, two games to go and very little hope left I'm afraid but I'm hanging on for a miracle." And like me Skeelo is an eternal optimist.

Mark Coupe was looking at a future in the Championship and wondering, if "anyone is up to following in Merson's footsteps?"

Guy Bailey, writing from 5,000 miles away in the USA asked, "how an up and coming, young English manager, appointed without qualifications against FA regulations and many fans' wishes; has taken a team which finished in Europe twice on the spin and so thoroughly dismantled it in the time since, that by the end of the fateful Newcastle match, it looked like a less organised Teesborough league side."

Friday 15th May 2009
Song for the day: Talk Talk – It's My Life (US 12" Mix)

Newcastle United

Michael Owen has been in the news again, this time for apparently planning to retire at the end of the season to concentrate on his horses. Shearer, however has since been on Sky Sports saying Owen will be playing in the Premier League next year, though not necessarily for us.

Owen looks likely to be missing tomorrow according to reports, as he has a groin strain. Whether this will keep him out next week too is unclear, but that could well mean we have seen him in a black and white shirt for the last time.

Middlesbrough

It was a disaster at St. James' Park, pure and simple. Events elsewhere seemed to be conspiring to give us a glimmer of an opening but then the door was firmly slammed shut. In all likelihood for good. It felt like ecstasy when Tuncay was celebrating that early goal but the mood soon turned to absolute despair.

I cannot summon any real hope anymore, too beaten down by it all now. I want to go out with a home victory and end that horrendous record-breaking run with an away win at West Ham. Whatever will be will be elsewhere. I'll leave the radios and iPhone updates to others but for me it is important to at least end this watershed season with more points.

A win against Villa means an unlikely double and also pay back for all those crushing defeats they have inflicted here over the years. It may not end up counting for much in the final table but it would likely as not take things into the last match. It would put Sunderland under pressure at Pompey knowing they have Chelsea to face last match. Listen to me; I'm getting carried away again.

The main thing is to win and put on a defiant show in this, possibly our last home Premier League game for a little while. The players and management owe it to the supporters to be professional and take it to the final 90 minutes. Then, well you never know. I suppose we have to savour everything we have left this campaign. No point in bowing out with a whimper, might as well show the world that we have Premier support. It's time to unite and make one last stand. If we are to go out then we must go out with a real fight.

Hoping for a miracle. Come on Boro.

Saturday 16th May 2009
Song for the day: The Smiths – How Soon Is Now?

Sunderland

Another weekend at work is had. There is good news in the form of a day's leave on Monday, to be able to take in the Portsmouth game live on Setanta – a game originally scheduled for today. Following the Everton circus act, I vowed not to watch Sunderland again whilst Sbragia remained in charge, it was then I remembered that unfortunately, no matter what other joys and vices there lies in modern society, SAFC will always play a major role in my days on earth, no matter what. A birthright? More like a life's burden. You can choose your friends, but one's football club is bestowed upon them (unless one is a plastic Liverpool/Chelsea/Manchester United fan).

With our game now kicking off on Monday, we will all know what is required come the kick-off and where we stand. Potentially, Sunderland could be home and dry without kicking a ball. On the other hand, we could also sit alarmingly in the bottom three, staring at the trapdoor of relegation. We require a Bolton victory over Hull, a Fulham away win at Sid James', Liverpool to pummel West Brom and Villa to play Boro off the park. I fancy a Bolton, Villa and Liverpool win, whether Fulham can pull it off remains to be seen.

Watching Football Focus my heart fills with dread. Close analysis on the bottom of the table reveals my biggest fears. They display the league table after potential wins for Hull and Newcastle today. It is an unnerving sight, Sunderland in the bottom three with two games to play. The biggest disappointment of it all (should these consequences play themselves true) was that it was Sunderland's to throw away, rather than any of their rivals playing well. Maybe they can rename the club – Shouldhaverland.

Manchester United 0 Arsenal 0

United win the league and there is hell on in the office. I am seriously worried that they will not take the Hull game seriously, whilst most of the co-workers in there including the officer in charge, all hate United and so have turned the coverage of the celebrations at Old Trafford over, opting for a Saturday afternoon matinee of 'Carry On Cleo' leaving me wondering whether to laugh or cry. Laugh as the film will save me from waves of anxiety all afternoon, clock watching the football, or cry as I will only give in to look up the scores via the internet, whilst putting up with this awful shite on the TV. Quite apt really, the relegation run in is akin to a Carry On film/pantomime.

I eventually take control of the office TV remote control and elect to switch over to Sky Sports News. Goals fly in, chances go begging and as I sit here, Hull are level at Bolton. Boro are 1-1 and the Mags are a goal down, with a man sent off. I pray for full time now, especially as Mark Viduka has had a goal chalked off. Ha'waaaaaaaay! I cannot bear it anymore.

Again, I am too excited to write, adrenalin racing through my veins, my hands shaking like a bad case of Parkinson's.

Full Time Scores
Newcastle United 0 Fulham 1
Middlesbrough 1 Aston Villa 1
Bolton Wanderers 1 Hull City 1

One cannot ask for any more than that. My nerves have yet to settle. I am sat at my desk perspiring, red faced and flustered. I require a stiff top shelf drink, when I finish this shift. My head is full of chaos and so I will refrain from writing, whilst I go and calm myself down.

Newcastle United

It's a big day today. Hull at Bolton, Boro vs. Villa, and the Toon at home to Fulham. Once again the permutations and possible outcomes are huge, with the chance of relegation issues being decided. Fingers crossed.

NUFC 0 – 1 Fulham

Disaster! Calamity! AAAAAAGGGGGGGHHHHHHHHHHH!

Typical bloody Newcastle. After hauling ourselves into a position where our destiny is in our own hands, the Toon go and blow it again at home. Awful defending for their goal, a huge blunder by the ref disallowing a Viduka 'goal' and then Bassong getting caught out by a long ball, resulting in a red card for a professional foul, then to add insult to injury, Hull and Boro both pick up a point, leaving us third bottom with one game to go.

The main talking point is Viduka's disallowed effort, the ref Mr Howard Webb (supposedly our best) asserting that Kevin Nolan had fouled Schwarzer in goal. Replays clearly show Nolan stands in front of the keeper, but when he tries to go past Nolan doesn't impede him in any way. Schwarzer is clear of Nolan when Viduka heads the ball and yet still the 'goal' is ruled out. I have played football and watched it all my life, and at practically every corner at every level of the game a player from the attacking side stands in front of the goalkeeper. Suddenly this is deemed to be against the rules. As far as I am aware, a player does not have to move out of the way for an opponent and is perfectly entitled to stand his ground. This could have won us the point, which staves off relegation. As it is we now have to do better than Hull next week, not simply match them.

Of course, the phrase what goes around comes around has been bandied about claiming Nolan impeded a Boro player for Taylor's goal last week, and also Mr

Webb awarded our penalty against Sunderland which gained us a point. My view on this – bollocks! Nuff said!

Middlesbrough

Boro 1 Aston Villa 1

At half time everyone believed in miracles. Five junior supporters clipped the frame of the goal to pass the crossbar challenge and go into a draw for season cards. Everyone was singing the theme from the Great Escape as Boro led at home, whilst Newcastle and Hull were down. If only we could have held on... if only, but no. In the end we ran out of legs and ideas as captain Downing was kicked off the park, football swift Gary O'Neill limped off and our last chance faded out of sight.

It had been a fantastic start. We sprung into action straight from the kick off, Downing's cross intercepted and almost run into the corner of the net. We played the attacking formation that would have been the choice of so many of the fans with Emnes again looking oh so lively and Tuncay a box of tricks beside him. Adam Johnson was asked to run the right wing; sadly he didn't have a head for heights.

It was a tremendous break away that gave us hope. Downing was picked out wide left and when his shot was blocked Tuncay acrobatically bicycle kicked the ball past Friedel and into the net. What a goal! What a start.

With Boro threatening to tear into Villa, then came the cynical challenge that probably ended our Premier reign. Downing tried to get up and twice tried to run it off but no use. Our captain and creative hub kicked out of a vital game. Am I right in thinking he had played every minute in the Premier League until then? It must be close if not. Will we ever see Stewart pull on the red and white shirt again?

This meant reorganising with Tuncay pushed back into midfield, O'Neill wide right and Johnson given the opportunity to prove himself an able successor to Stewy. Johnno was soon nobbled as well dribbling at speed into the area and Boro now lacked the balance and cutting edge we had enjoyed earlier. Sub Marlon King held the ball up manfully but Boro had lost real cohesion.

Still, we had opportunities to add to our lead, Emnes dribbled the ball along the goal line and pulled it back for Hoyte whose shot was only just clawed away. At our end Brad Jones was playing well and Huth and Wheater defended like lions, whilst Arca recalled from nowhere refused to lie down as he harried and hustled and harried some more, all afternoon long.

The Villa goal came after a period of pressure from them and an almighty scramble that we couldn't clear. The ball was on a string and refused to leave our box until Carew snuck the ball home to break our hearts and more or less end our resistance to relegation. The cartoon fancy dress of Villa fans set off in a conga. Three pink panthers, ten Scooby doos, a couple of supermen and an Adolf Hitler led the way. Somehow I think Adolf misread the mood.

Jones made an incredible save at the feet of Ashley Young. Wheater and Huth were so brave in holding on against Villa ram raids. At the other end we couldn't work an opening. When O'Neill the metronome of the side limped off you knew we were in all sorts of trouble.

Hull had equalised at Bolton, now it was serious. Newcastle were down to 10 men - serious for them too. Could we possibly summon one last effort? No, sadly the inexperience of the players showed and with so many of our better players injured in Downing, Alves, O'Neill and Digard, there just wasn't the ability to smuggle a winning goal. Some of the young players showed they still haven't quite got the resources to cope with the situation. We were on a knife-edge and we couldn't turn it into our opponents.

At the end the players slumped to the ground. There was applause, cheers for Tuncay and Alves, boos, coupled with expletives for Southgate. Then we turned to leave the ground knowing the road is now onwards and downwards into the Championship. Only the miracle of a goal fest at West Ham can save us and when do we ever end the season by scoring several goals in a game? Doh! Middlesbrough 8-1 Man City – last game 2007-08, but not this time me thinks. Goodbye Chelsea, Plymouth here we come.

Sunday 17th May 2009
Song for the day: Thievery Corporation (feat. LouLou) – La Femme Parallel

Sunderland

West Bromwich Albion 0 Liverpool 2

Another cracking result goes Sunderland's way and Albion are relegated. Two places still mathematically up for grabs, even though Boro need to win by four goals or Hull to lose by four, it is a tall order and considering the Smogs can't catch us, Sunderland really only need to avoid the final relegation place. It is now a direct battle between Hull, the Mags and us and if we win at Fratton Park tomorrow we're with the big boys for another season.

Away from tomorrow's game, other fans have turned their attentions towards the Aston Villa vs Newcastle game next Sunday. A new badge has been designed incorporating the current Villa badge, transforming the claret and blue with the red and white of Sunderland and 'Ha'way the Lads' and 'fuck Newcastle' written underneath. I feel it is a piece of work truly with the concept of modern art in mind and it is worthy of being short listed for the Turner Prize, although somehow I don't think this will be noted. There is even talk of fans travelling to Villa Park to witness first hand the demise of Newcastle United.

Personally, I would rather concentrate my energy on my own team (also in a bout of crisis) before commenting on others, with this attention starting at Fratton Park tomorrow night. Everything is in place for a Sunderland victory, even Pompey are safe, surely they'll let us win! In the back of my mind, I fear the lines will be fluffed by the team in a catastrophic manner that only Sunderland can muster.

Newcastle United

Still can't believe we blew it – again. Okay, Fulham are going pretty well in the league under Roy Hodgson, but does anyone really think they are a good side? They are a decent side yes, but not good. How many of their current players would you hope to sign. Murphy? Bullard? Bring Aaron Hughes back? Yet we still can't score against them at SJP. If teams such as Fulham, West Ham, Man City, Everton and Villa are amongst the best in the land, maybe the Premier League isn't as great as we think it is. Take away the top four and what exactly are you left with? Not a great deal in my humble opinion.

Middlesbrough

I'm now writing from within a black cloud, relegation gloom has well and truly descended. There was an incredible atmosphere at West Brom. The crowd did everything they could to Boing Boing their team to success and all in vain. It wasn't quite like that at the Riverside but it has been a long, slow protracted death this season and had simply drained the lifeblood out of everyone.

The West Brom crowd today reminds me of our final home game of the 96/97 season. We were on the verge of relegation and guess what? It was against Aston Villa. Inspired by the crowd we fought back for a draw and faint hopes of survival. It seems a long, long time ago now.

Mind you there was no booing on Saturday or mass protests. Some fans had called for action, but for better or for worse it won't happen now.

Monday 18th May 2009
Song for the day: Thomas P. Heckman – Amphetamine (Original)

Sunderland

I am offered the option of Monday night football for a change and this means I have the luxury of popping over the road onto camp and watching the game, as apparently one of the bars there has subscribed to Setanta…

… 'We only do channels with the numbers 1 to 5 I'm afraid' was the unnerving answer I didn't want to hear from my original question of 'are you showing the match?' With one bar completely shut and the other about as much use as tits on fish, I was in trouble and confined to the idea of an emergency trip to Wootton Bassett, with the match already underway. Shit!

The Waggon and Horses was finally reached fifteen minutes into the game, the barman kindly informing me (he had already identified me as the mad Mackem at the showing of the Newcastle vs Sunderland derby in February) that Peter Crouch had hit the bar, although Sunderland were the more dominant side. This information I could do without I replied, thinking he was only trying to divert me to the top shelf as soon as possible in a bid to raise more revenue for his bar.

A pint of Guinness was ordered and a nice blackcurrant and soda for our lass (the driver) and it was down to the professional business of watching Sunderland AFC.

Portsmouth 3 Sunderland 1 - Initial Thoughts

Having just returned from Bassett, I am now resigned to packing the whole football-supporting lark in. There seems to be no highs anymore, not that it was ever about that following Sunderland.

The modern game is dominated by under achieving, money grabbing con artists, who are nothing short of mercenaries. I work with loyal soldiers serving their country and I support a team that contains soldiers... of fortune, loyal only to the banknote.

I guess Sunderland AFC is my affliction in life, which by the going rate is not too bad. Some are born into the third world, some born into poverty. Some are born with illnesses and some of us are born to support fucking Sunderland AFC.

This feels like the final nail in the coffin for my supporting career, but it's hard to give up. I have invested 30 years of my life into Sunderland AFC – emotions, time and money, all used following my local side, who are the epitome of my city. I must feel like the Labour government and the continued assault in Afghanistan. Both of us are at a crossroads, both have invested so much into our own campaigns... do we jump ship and cut our losses, or in my case an umbilical chord, or do we stay and fight, potentially suffering further upset, that could still redeem itself and turn out for the best?

To be honest I am tired of it all. I am past raising my hopes, sick of suffering abject performances. The thing is I don't know what else to do. Football has been everything, though when it boils down to the preservation of 'normal' life, I suppose things must change, if not only to keep my sanity. Perhaps I will become a nicer person, without the added pressures of watching eleven pampered babies, overpaid tossers, who can not control a ball with their first touch, do not understand how to hit a target from five yards and certainly have not the skill to trap the proverbial bag of cement.

Or maybe I should merely divert my football attentions elsewhere and concentrate on forming an alliance of fan football, or be resolute in remembering the pre-Sky days of football, when everything was basic and the distance between fan and player was only in how much further along the street the two lived.

Fuck 'em all, fuck 'em all,
Platini, Jimmy Hill and all,
We'll never be mastered by football authority bastards,
Cos the fans are the best of 'em all.

List of alternatives to Football	Tick Yes or No & add comments
Rugby Union	X – Not my scene
Formula One	X – Watching cars go round in a loop?
Tennis	X – Only like watching Wimbledon
Golf	X – Bored to tears
Cricket	X – Rather go to war
Playing on computers	X – Bunch of nerds
Go backpacking	X – Would be arrested for going AWOL
Write a book	X – Without football what would I write?
Skiing	X – No snow
Horse Racing	X – Gamble too much
Go to the gym	X – Trying to rid myself of prima donnas
Dogging	X – Don't fancy Syphilis
Go to the pub	X – Would become a plonky
Take the cats for a walk	X – The blighters would run away

And so anything that enters my head as a plan to remove myself from the confines of football is immediately followed by a negative response, akin to having a good angel and a devil sitting in either ear, battling away for control of your mind.

Football it is then…for now.

Newcastle United

All the Mackems at work were gloating today saying how we are down and the oh-so-wonderful Sunderland team will win tonight and be safe. Didn't quite work like that did it lads? A collapse very similar to the SAFC 1-4 NUFC game occurred when after taking the lead, the red and white cats shot themselves in the foot, or is that paws? Within a minute a Mackem headed the ball back into his own box where Utaka finished. (I did think the ref had blown before the goal though – hey ho!). The £8m defender Ant Ferdinand missed the ball and it was

2-1, then in the last moments, Sunderland failed to make a tackle and it was 3-1. Oh, shame about Jones hitting the post in the first half! Welcome to our world.

POS	TEAM	PLAYED	GD	POINTS
15	BLACKBURN	37	-20	40
16	MACKEMS	37	-19	36
17	HULL	37	-24	35
18	NEWCASTLE	37	-18	34
19	SMOGGIES	37	-28	32
20	BAGGIES	37	-31	31

Middlesbrough

Sunderland lose again. Typical, as I thought 37 points would have been enough to stay up. How on earth did we manage to get so few points? Even one win this month could have been enough.

Tuesday 19th May 2009
Song for the day: Fat Boy Slim – Going Out Of My Head

Sunderland

Why does no one believe me when I say that I have had it with Sunderland? On my Facebook status I declared that *'Mal Robinson has had enough of supporting Sunderland after 30 years of heartbreaks and disappointments... I'm too tired for it all. A sad, sad day indeed.'* The feedback and comments from others on the site do not appreciate the seriousness of it all, adding *'you'll be OK', 'the Mags and Hull won't win at the weekend'* and even some writing humorous comments stating *'I blame Hesford (SAFC's burly 1980s Goalkeeper with protruding facial hair), the rot has set in'.* Cheers Steven Douglas... just when I need comforting and counselling, I get laughter and banter. I'll remember!

Does no one realise that Sunderland AFC and I are on the rocks, on the verge of a massive split?

Fair enough, Sunderland may be fine, if other results go to plan, but that's not the point here. I am pig sick of it all, the ominous perilous falls at the final hurdle with the winning line in sight, the reliance on others to help us out of a sticky situation, the lack of effort and foresight, the wrong appointments, false dawns, no character, no skill, no passion, caught daydreaming, wondering what on earth you are doing sat here watching this shit, the worry, the constant analysing of the league relegation zone, the public mocking, the patronising comments from inside the club and the associated press, the flash-in-the-pan highs – followed almost immediately by the mind numbing, skull crushing blows – the whole package gift wrapped in black, red and white colours, complete with a gift tag reading 'Dear Supporter, please be advised that the club are doing everything within our power to ensure that success is only around the corner and therefore we endeavour to provide you, the fans, with a club and platform of football to be proud of. P.S. Season ticket renewals are due in by the end of May, otherwise you've lost your seat.'

Well, I have marked my package 'RETURN TO SENDER', whether or not I will go the whole mile and post it back remains to be seen.

Portsmouth 3 Sunderland 1 – The Match Verdict

The match itself started off brightly as it so often does with us. I had missed Peter Crouch's header off the woodwork for the hosts, due to the inconvenience of travelling to Wootton Bassett.

Sunderland moved the ball better than in previous weeks, utilising both full backs to good effect and when Kieran Richardson and Steed Malbranque both squandered great chances, it was only to be a matter of time before we broke the deadlock. Kenwyne Jones' superb header off the post was reinforcing Sunderland's intent and as half time sounded we felt it somewhat unjust that it was still 0-0.

The second half though fell apart before our eyes, despite taking the lead through excellent work from my man of the match Calum Davenport, who ran down the right flank and steered in a classic first time ball for Jones to prod home. It was a cross that the likes of David Beckham and Ronaldo would have been proud of, never mind our so-called wingers.

I celebrated with half of the pub, united in my cause of Wearside allegiance, most likely in reality to do with the bets they had placed beforehand.

The whole place was quiet though within 90 seconds; Pompey equalizing through slack play from Sunderland. Referee Alan Wiley had appeared to blow up before the ball hit the net, before changing his mind, allowing the goal to stand. It was something Setanta concentrated on for the remainder of the game.

Some Sunderland fans I dare say would follow suit, surely after some injustice under the headlines of… 'How Alan Wiley sent Sunderland down!' Personally, I thought there was no evidence of any wrong doing from Pompey players, if not then it was our own group of stars that may have forced the referee's whistle, with a shove in the back of Crouch from Anton Ferdinand. Couple that with Grant Leadbitter's inability to control the ball, handing possession back to the home team to score their leveller.

Ferdinand had an even larger part to play in Pompey's second. Unable to trap a rabbit riddled with mixer mitosis, the centre half allowed a routine long ball to slip under his feet, the ball rolling to the centre forward who gleefully took the ball around the advancing Fulop, only for the onrushing Phil Bardsley to race back and take the ball off the striker, whilst inadvertently stroking the ball home into his own net. A farcical and embarrassing comedy of errors, which did not look out of place in the lower leagues – a place Sunderland will inevitably be heading on this showing.

The calamitous second Portsmouth goal reminded me of Sunderland's Official History video I once owned on VHS. It contained highlights (?) of the Lads playing at Plough Lane – home of Wimbledon FC, in an FA Cup encounter around the time we were on a downward spiral in the mid-Eighties, eventually resulting in relegation to Division Three. This was a cup tie in January, probably the third round stage, as Sunderland never got beyond that ever – apart from 1973 and 1992. Wimbledon's killer goal showed the frail Sunderland defence at sixes and sevens, all over the place, being dragged all over the shop, twisting and turning, trying to cover each other's howling mistakes. For 1986 read 2009 and Fratton Park instead of South London. Replace the likes of Steve Hetzke and Steve Doyle with Anton Ferdinand and Phil Bardsley and things look just as bleak as they did back then.

Pompey scored another at the death and that was that. Eventually, Sbragia brought on another forward to help Jones in the form of the soon to be departing Djibril Cisse – this with a mere 14 minutes left to play. And then the icing on the cake, when with a few minutes remaining Sbragia made his third and final change. Off came the hapless Leadbitter for… Daryl fucking Murphy.

Someone in the pub behind me jokingly remarked… 'Who's that? He looks like Niall Quinn's son!' At least now I know why the fucker gets a game at Sunderland. There must be no other explanation. Finally, someone has uncovered the truth behind the five-year contract given to Murphy, when there was no manager at the helm, in the pre-Roy Keane days at the SOL.

Now that that particular mystery was solved by Wiltshire's answer to Poirot, another one evolved in the same moment Murphy's number was displayed at pitch side. Just what has David Healy deserved to be left out to rot on the bench, never seemingly offered a chance to shine and succumbing to the final embarrassment – behind Daryl Murphy in the pecking order of the team. Surely David Healy MBF, that's MBE, awarded for his services to international football with Northern Ireland, deserves a crack of the whip up front? He is Ireland's record goal scorer after all for God's sake.

So then down to the last day of the season… again. Why do we always leave it to now to settle an issue? Will Sunderland survive? Do I care anymore?

At least my Newcastle-supporting friend Graeme H left us alone last night. It is really saying something when neither set of Sunderland or Newcastle fans can take the Michael and poke fun, with both teams as bad as each other. I think we are both not in the mood, but I would be lying if I did not say I'd celebrate if they went down, having grown up in the shadow of the Keegan era at Tyneside, whilst we suffered relentlessly watching teams under the control of Terry Butcher and Mick Buxton, coupled with the threats of turning Newcastle into the new Barcelona of the North East under Sir John Hall.

In the words of Kevin Keegan… 'I'd love it, LOVE IT, if we beat them'. Ha ha.

Sky Sports have announced they are showing three live matches on what they have dubbed *'Survival Sunday'.* I would prefer to call it *'Shit my pants Sunday'* or at least *'Squeaky Bum Sunday'* but I can't see that being approved in the PC world of today's society. It would prove to make an interesting advertising campaign I feel.

TV Man's Voiceover: 'Live, this weekend…Sunderland, Newcastle and Hull face the battle to avoid the drop. Fasten your seatbelts and bring out the Huggies… it's Shit Your Pants Sunday… Live only on Sky Sports 2. You've got to be in it to shit it!'

Well something along those lines would suffice. In reality, I will be at work, sat precariously in the office. I opted to work, firmly believing that Sunderland would have by now had a word with themselves, realised they were massively under performing and done the deed of acquiring enough points for safety. What a bloody mug I am. Now I face the prospect of trying somehow to concentrate on work, whilst keeping one eye on all the scores. I hope the boss takes pity on me and sends me home for everyone's sake. I could take a sickie, but I have been offered the chance of representing the RAF the next day at Wembley to watch the Play-Off final between Burnley and Sheffield United. I may take a notebook along to record some notes to form some sort of guidance for Sunderland next season. Which team to cover depends on our own outcome the day before.

A nightmare scenario come Sunday then and here I was hoping to enjoy a relegation party for the Mags.

Newcastle United

It appears that the games featuring us, the Mackems, the Smogs and Hull will all be televised on Sunday. I am away this weekend with the Thomas Wilson FC annual trip (Huddersfield this year), but we are stopping at Ripon to watch the game on Sunday afternoon. Big mix of clubs between us so it could well be a highly emotional day!

The Sun printed a "hilarious" poem today to the words of The Blaydon Races, describing in detail Newcastle's relegation. Would be an awful shame if Scumderland went down. I wonder if the humorous scribe would re-write a verse or two telling of their demise?

Middlesbrough

Look I don't really want to write this thing anymore. We're down barring a miracle, Well, several miracles. I don't know that there will be much call for a relegation diary on Teesside, perhaps there would be on Wearside and Humberside/Tyneside at this rate.

Wednesday 20th May 2009

Song for the day: Chicane (feat. Salt Tank) – Leaving Town

Newcastle United

Not much to do but wait for the weekend. Owen and Baye are doubtful at the moment and Andy Carroll (who has put the effort in when on the pitch) is crocked until next season. A point should do it, but Manchester United are making noises about putting a very weakened side out against Hull City – if they actually have a weak side that is. Chances are most of their reserves and juniors are better than most other first team squads.

Middlesbrough

Tonight Alastair Brownlee interviewed two sets of Boro walkers on BBC Tees. George Cooke and his gang from Middlesbrough FC in the Community were scaling the Cumbrian fells on their way across the country. Meanwhile a band of intrepid Boro fans were walking the length of the country for charity. For the final game of the 2007-2008-football season Paul Brand, Rob Blanchard and Jeff Patterson completed a charity walk from the Eagle pub in Eaglescliffe to the Riverside Stadium in Middlesbrough. After the walk's success they pledged a repeat for the final match of this season. Little did they know that it would be away to West Ham United! Get your hiking boots on then boys.

The lads set off from the Riverside straight after the Villa game heading south for London. A gallon of money had already been raised for the Finlay Cooper Fund, Bobby Moore Fund and NSPCC.

Thursday 21st May 2009
Song for the day: The Chemical Brothers – Let Forever Be

Newcastle United

Last day at work until Tuesday so the final chance for a bit of Geordie-Mackem banter with the lads. Everyone is worried about going down, and confidence is low across the board. I still think we will get a point but will it be enough?

Middlesbrough

Boro fans' group the Twe12th Man are appealing to supporters to help create two new banners for the Riverside by donating old Boro away shirts and those of the club's former UEFA Cup opponents. The press release reads as follows:

"The Twe12th Man have started to collect unwanted Boro away shirts from over the years as well as the replicas of Boro's 17 opponents from the club's UEFA Cup campaigns.

The shirts will be sewn together to form new colorful banners which will be displayed at the Riverside next season as a permanent reminder of the club's recent past."

Sickening and sobering to think how far we have fallen since those heady days. From Sevilla to Swansea in three short seasons.

Friday 22nd May 2009
Song for the day: Friendly Fires – Jump In My Pool.

Sunderland

I have kept myself busy all week, trying to avoid the topic of football, so busy in fact I forgot it was Friday and the beginning of the weekend, the beginning of the build up to 'Shit Yer Pants Sunday', the beginning of the end? I now cannot wait any longer.

I bumped into a Geordie lad – Gav Barr – who is off to Villa on Sunday to support the Mags. I feel a slight sense of guilt that I am not present at the SOL in two days' time. As I put it to him though, it is Newcastle's first relegation battle in 17 years. It is our umpteenth and I'm tired and weary.

Still tonight I relax listening to a bit of quality atmospheric Friendly Fires tunes. I look outside into the glittering night sky, gaze down the street, now empty and still for this dark hour and see a small Black Cat crossing the road. An omen? Good or perhaps bad (never cross a Black Cat)… methinks good this time, just a feeling that on this occasion, the luck is with us.

Newcastle United

I am off to Huddersfield on the football team trip. Only nineteen of us this year, but on Sunday we are being joined in Ripon for the match by some lads who are in Blackpool for the weekend, and a car-full of lads are driving down from Gateshead to meet up and watch the match, just to be there in support of the lads.

Middlesbrough

It's almost the end of the line now, but not before I've done a few interviews from the other end of a phone line. I had to be up early doors for a Radio 5 Live interview. I have tried to put a brave face on it, a bit of fighting talk, but come on we need something very special to happen now. Probably divine intervention. Enter mad Boro fan Father Paul Farrer, also interviewed on another mobile line from Teesside Airport on his way to Lourdes. He'll be praying for our survival he says.

In the afternoon, I am phoned by both Sky Sports News and Sky News. Survival Sunday is big news now. We are only just clinging on in there but while we still technically have a chance there is media interest. I do a piece for Sky Sports and then Sky News ask me if I can hop round to St. James' Park to be interviewed with a Newcastle and Sunderland fan. I explain to the London-based researcher that Newcastle is not just round the corner. He then asks about Durham, I explain that too is a long walk. Do they not teach geography in Southern schools?

Anyhow, Sky dispatched a taxi to take me to the Durham studio, which is right next to Durham City football ground and a centre-back clearance away from the fantastically named Dragonville. I held a live interview to the camera shown on Sky News. Quite exciting. I can't see there being much call for this kind of thing next season. Once again I talked as if survival was still possible. The Newcastle fan seems to think they will do the stuff at Villa Park. Not so sure myself. I do reckon most of the relegation candidates will lose. If Man United reserves can cane Hull then we might have a slim chance, nothing more.

Saturday 23rd May 2009
Song for the day: Elbow – Grounds for Divorce

Sunderland

One day to go. All the battle cries have been sounded. All the pundits have cast their vote on which clubs will survive tomorrow. There are no more words to be spoken. It is Saturday and it is strangely quiet on the football front, with only a Play-Off final and the Scottish Premier League taking place.

It is also Bank Holiday weekend and I am at bloody work. Tomorrow has already been earmarked to spend 90 minutes away from civilisation in case I turn into the Hulk or some other type of monster. I shall plaster 'KEEP AWAY' signs all over my desk and body. No form of communication can be had with the outside world whilst 'Shit Yer Pants Sunday' is underway.

Theories, predictions and concepts overwhelm fans' forums, personal texts and newspaper columns. It is the most exciting finish in years to a Premier League season and we are right in the thick of it. I pray for a quick release tomorrow, or a good spanking for the Mags to set us all at ease, but of course it will not be that simple. It will last until the final minute of the last kick of this dire season to decide each club's fate.

Newcastle United

Twenty four hours and counting to Survival Sunday as Sky Sports are calling it. The bookies reckon Boro and Newcastle will complete the bottom three, and they don't often get it wrong, so that's a bad omen. Bugger! My brother is putting on a bet for the entire bottom five to get beat. He could be right – which would be curtains for us.

Middlesbrough

I take a walk over the new Infinity Bridge in Stockton. Miserable weather and a miserable day. Our last day in the Premier most likely. How long before we are back in the top flight? I hope it is not an infinite length of time...

There has been so much talk this week about Man United's team at Hull City. The way Phil Brown's side is playing even the Red Devils' youth team should be able to take them apart. We must go for it at West Ham. I can't feel nervous anymore because I don't believe any longer. We need to go down with a fight. Having defeated West Ham quite recently we have to believe that at least is possible. We must end this appalling record-breaking away run. Something positive before the season is out, please. Funny things can happen in the last match...

Sunday 24th May 2009 – 'Shit Yer Pants Sunday'

Song for the day: Sunderland – A Love Supreme - Niall Quinn's Disco Pants Are The Best / Take That – Perfect Day (Live at The Stadium of Light)
Newcastle United – Geordie Ridley - The Blaydon Races
Middlesbrough: Perfecto Allstarz - Reach Up (Papa's Got A Brand New Pigbag)
Hull City: Mud - Tiger Feet

Sunderland

D-Day has arrived! Survival Sunday, Saviour Sunday, Sick Sunday, Shit Yer Pants Sunday, or whatever else people have labelled it.

It is 08.00, I'm at work and the place is buzzing. All everyone is talking about is the North East three. Even lads with no interest in football are passing comment, joining in with the banter, even if they are off the pace a little.

'Let us take the piss out of Scott, he's a Mag', I say

'No he supports Newcastle' comes the uneducated response!

At least they have involved themselves in the world's greatest game for once in their sorry lives.

My head is pounding already – it is definitely a stress headache, arching behind the eye socket, gently stabbing away like a mountaineer slashing away at frozen slopes of ice with their pick, until eventually the pain becomes almost unbearable. A simple closing of the eyes eases the symptoms, but they are back out in force when I concentrate on the games ahead, eyes closed or not.

The fans' forum is going bananas for this time of day on a Bank Holiday Sunday morning. Threads covering everything imaginable relating to today's action. I found the piece about the best way to keep up to date with the scores whilst attending the game was of a most fascinating read. Phone calls, portable radios, internet on the mobile phone, word of mouth, racing pigeon, scoreboard, the manager's tactics at half time, message in a bottle – they have all been cited. This reminds me that I will be the first port of call to relay scores to brother-in-law Al and the lads at the SOL today, a role of significant importance. It leaves no room for pranks or any tomfoolery 'despite his wind up in Dublin; crucial key information is vital to the cause and can affect the fans' mood inside the ground reflecting in turn upon the team's performance.

I have asked our lass to record Soccer Saturday or rather Soccer Sunday; in case I cannot take the pain of watching the events unfold live. This has since backfired as everyone in the operations room wants to watch me squirm and so they have elected to watch every drop of action from the TV screen as it happens. Bugger.

The fact that last night I only enjoyed three or four hours sleep is starting to catch up on me. I am slacking slightly, the emotion of it all pushing me nearer to the edge… of what I just don't know.

Back online, rumours are abound that the M6 motorway is closed southbound into the direction of Birmingham and therefore the Villa/Newcastle game may be delayed, giving them the advantage of knowing what is required after all the other scores have crept in. It reminds many fans of the Coventry City saga back in 1977, when allegedly, then City Chairman Jimmy Hill delayed their kick off to enable the Sky Blues and opponents Bristol City to play out a goal-less draw, knowing about Sunderland's defeat at Goodison Park and therefore our imminent demise, to keep both sides in the top flight. Sunderland perished as a consequence of a last day delayed kick off again in 1997, as Sunderland took over 10,000 away fans to Selhurst Park, Wimbledon; Coventry's game at White Hart

Lane, Spurs, was delayed due to crowd congestion, when they only took 3,000 fans. Coventry had their game delayed again, leaving us in attendance over the other side of the capital foaming with a nasty taste in the mouth. I suppose it is accepted to have slight bouts of paranoia about delaying tactics come the last day having had our fingers burnt twice in the past.

Still, news arrives that a number of people have been killed in that said crash and so people are duly reminded that a little respect is required in all this.

Shit Yer Pants Sunday's Drunken Conclusion

Can't speak... too drunk... too emotional... will need to have a sit down and gather my thoughts... I can't take it all in... too drunk... it's nearly midnight... just back from a booze filled session at Big Ecky's house... we fight to live another Premiership day... as do Hull City meaning the darkness has subsided.

More to follow... unable to function.

Newcastle United

Judgement Day. The Hornblower pub in Ripon is the venue for the match, with a cross section of teams. Probably about 60% Newcastle, 30% Sunderland and a few Boro and Hull fans in there too, just for good measure.

Aston Villa 1 – 0 NUFC

The worst-case scenario happened. A heartless finish to the season, another blank in the goals scored column and relegation with the Smogs and West Brom. Hull got beat off Manchester United reserves, Sunderland lost to Chelsea, Boro lost at West Ham and so a draw would have done us. The bad luck, which has contributed to our failings, continued with the Villa goal deflecting off Damien Duff and wrong-footing Harper in goal. Despite a certain lack of effort by Villa, we simply didn't create any real chances. With 20 minutes left we should have been throwing the kitchen sink at Villa but there seemed to be a resigned air about most of the players.

So, it's goodbye Man Utd, Arsenal, Liverpool and all and hello to Doncaster, Blackpool and Scunthorpe, on the plus side we are already 7-2 with the bookies to win the league. Just time now for the aftermath.

On 13th April I made a prediction how the bottom six would finish, so here it is with correct totals:

TEAM		CURRENT POINTS	PREDICTED POINTS
	BLACKBURN	34	42
	NEWCASTLE	30	38
	SUNDERLAND	32	36
R	HULL	34	35
R	MIDDLESBROUGH	30	31
R	WEST BROM	25	27

In the end I was pretty close, with only my miss-placed optimism about us spoiling things. The actual bottom of the table in all its glory (or gory) looks like this:

POS	TEAM	PLAYED	GD	POINTS
16	MACKEMS	38	-20	36
17	HULL	38	-25	35
18	NEWCASTLE	38	-19	34
19	SMOGGIES	38	-29	32
20	BAGGIES	38	-31	32

The Aftermath

It's strange, but maybe because the players seemed so resigned to relegation after Villa's goal, I think I may have accepted it rather quickly and more easily than I should (i.e. as soon as the final whistle went!). Obviously all the Mackems have been trying to wind me up since my return to work, but as yet they haven't actually got to me.

I now just look at it as a chance to get rid of the dross, rebuild the structure of the club and start again. The phoenix rising from the ashes! The attempts by my friends from the village down the A19 to rile me, and get me to bite at their sniping, really isn't working (despite what they would claim)

Maybe as a member of the older generation of fans who have seen all this before in the 70s and 80s means that I can accept it easier? I am not saying that I am not disappointed and angry at being let down on and off the pitch by my club, but I have managed to avoid the sense of heartbreak and desolation that that the supporters who appear in the newspapers crying into their scarves seem to feel. Does this mean I am not a true fan, and don't really care? Or does this mean I am a complete fan and will support my side through the bad times as well as the good with the same unswerving loyalty? Maybe that is for other people to judge.

I think that I, along with most right-thinking football fans, know that we are a BIG club. Ok, we haven't won a trophy in my lifetime, but is it simply silverware that makes a club big? Or is it other things as well? The fan base and passion of the supporters? The history of the club? The importance of the club in its geographical context? The view of the club by others? The recognition of the club across the country and the globe? The players who have represented the club?

So next season we will be in the Championship, or Division Two - whatever you wish to call it, while the Premier League (or old fashioned Division One) will be graced by the likes of Wigan, Hull, Burnley, Fulham, Stoke and Sunderland. Are these bigger clubs than Newcastle? Sunderland certainly have a fan base and support to rival most. Burnley and Stoke have a history as top clubs with top players in the past (Stanley Matthews anyone?). Wigan and Hull have bigger rugby sides than football, but have gained the points to stay in the top division.

Being honest though, who do you think will gain the most newspaper column inches next season? Who will fans across the country be talking about and keeping an eye on the progress of? Who will have the biggest average crowd? Who will be on Sky Sports and Setanta and Football Focus etc more than the others? Who will have the biggest away support and sell the most tickets around the country? Chances are, it will be Newcastle United as the answer to all the above.

Does this, however give us a divine right to be up with the elite? Absolutely and categorically not. Big club or not, you must earn the right to whatever you achieve as a club on the pitch. Newcastle did not do enough this season to stay up, and so will be ranked alongside Peterborough, Swansea, Scunthorpe and Ipswich next season. We will have other "big" clubs with history alongside us such as Sheffield United, West Brom, Preston North End and further down the ladder are Mighty Leeds, still languishing in League One (Old Division Three?) and are certainly a big club by all the criteria I have applied to Newcastle.

So what does the future hold now? Firstly we need to employ a manager who is strong enough to take control of the whole set up of the club and allow him to restructure as he sees fit. He needs to be given time to improve things, not just throw money at an overnight fix that will collapse within a year or two. Whether that man will be or should be Alan Shearer is open to debate. Whether the man paying him is Mike Ashley, Prince Aba Lottadosh, Ivan Afootieclub or Chuck McYankee doesn't matter, as long as he does things right and knows (or comes to know) the importance of Newcastle United Football Club to the entire region, not just the city itself.

I see no reason why Newcastle can not bounce back at the first attempt, once we have jettisoned some of the players whose hearts never really seemed to be at the club, or those who simply didn't work out and play to their best each and every game. Out the door I expect to see Coloccini, Owen, Viduka, Casapa, Smith, Barton, Martins, Lovenkrands, Geremi, Xisco, Gonzalez (who?) and maybe Bassong. Players I would like to stay because they would be as good as anything else in the division and could help us up include Taylors (Ryan and Steven), Nolan, Duff, Carroll, Beye, Enrique, Ameobi, Ranger, Harper and Guthrie. With that nucleus and a couple of pacey strikers/wingers and a ball-playing midfielder, as well as cover at full back and an experienced centre back and I think we should be challenging to come straight back up.

Whatever happens, you can guarantee things in and around St James' Park will never, ever be dull, and the Geordie faithful will back their club to the hilt. Auf Wiedersehen Lads, but I expect to be seeing you back real soon. Wye Aye man!

Middlesbrough

Here it is, our date with destiny. On the train down there are a few Corus employees who were talking about how they will struggle to fund away trips next season. They're wondering where they will get work; this puts it all into context again.

I bumped into MFC communications chief Dave Allan on the tube together with Eric Paylor and Anthony Vickers of the Gazette. Anthony Vickers broke the news that there will be an additional 2,000 miles to travel to all the away matches next season. Good grief! Dave Allan told us that the club had requested to the Football League that our Plymouth away game should be on a weekend. Small mercies perhaps.

I met the boro2upton walkers outside West Ham's quaint ground; they were just approaching as I arrived at the turnstiles. What a fantastic effort. I hope they at least get to witness Boro bowing out with a win. Then who knows what might happen. Don't get your hopes up; there lies the path to madness.

After the match

Boro without Downing, a taste of the future perhaps. Unfortunately I wouldn't say Adam Johnson did anything to indicate he will step into Stewy's shoes. It was a reasonable performance by Boro in the first half without really looking like we could win let alone slaughter them, as we needed to. Gary O'Neill was head and shoulders above most of our players. Tuncay was also a cut above but far more the individual than O'Neill the team player. If only we had a few more. If only Gary had been more consistent himself throughout this season.

The eventual West Ham goal was an absolute sickener, no question about that. Another instance where our defence was pulled around and an opponent allowed to steal in to stick a knife in the wound. Boro fans responded by singing ever more loudly. If we were to go down we would do it with pride.

In the second half Gary O'Neill capped his superman performance with a deserved goal. A glimmer of hope at last. Everyone else seemed to be losing. Could we now push on to get into a winning position and then see if Hull might capitulate under the pressure? No. Brad Jones should not have been beaten by a long distance effort. Poor. That sinking feeling again. This time there was no way back. Gary O'Neill had run out of pitch and ended up in the crowd, his legs were gone now. Bring on the young subs; Franks joined Bennett on the pitch.

In times of adversity we traditionally turn to the Boro hymn "We shall overcome someday. Oh deep in my heart I do believe we shall overcome Sunday." It was moving and at the same time inspiring, however there was also gallows humour in the away end, "We're all going to Blackpool." It was almost sung in celebration. Then gradually the time started to slip through our fingers. The end of Boro Premier time and no longer anything we could do about it. The final whistle. Tears. Boro players collapsing before coming over to the fans. Shirts, boots etc thrown into the supporters. A few more tears shed here and there. Applause everywhere. Then came the confirmation. "The Geordies are down," someone shouted. A roar of delight seized the entire end. We were down but at least we were not going down alone. Weird scenes – some celebrating, some gutted. Some like me leaving in silence, head down, thinking of past relegations. Why do they always happen away from home? Thinking of how bright the prospects seemed back in August but how deep was the trough of despair now. Thinking, what now? The congested fixtures of the Championship. The long miles on the road. The midweek games. The pressures of knowing we have to escape. At least the Geordies will be with us. In the end though, does that really matter?

Hull City

After 104 years of never tasting top-flight football, my football team Hull City had finally made it into the top flight of English football. After years of grief and banter from all of my friends, telling me how 'Hull City were not good enough' and 'Hull City will never make it,' a remarkable 38th minute volley from our own Dean Windass not only gave us the lead in the biggest game of our existence, but gave Hull the biggest victory in our existence, in the Play-Off final at Wembley, May 2008. 'Small fry' Hull City was now a big fish Barclays Premier League team – who would have thought it?

My first taste of Premier League football started on the island of Cyprus. Sat in a bar on holiday, my father and I missed the first game of the season, but as this was the Premier League, the game would be screened live in the bar. Hull City had picked up their first top-flight fixture against Fulham. It wasn't too long before we began to chat to some Fulham supporters who had congregated and had started to mention the 'cricket score' they would mount up against a team that had never played a Premier League fixture before. After only a few minutes this became a reality as Fulham scored and our team were now behind. Tensions began to mount until Geovanni produced a left footed strike that brought the game level. This was a huge shock to everybody but the biggest shock was yet to come, as Hull City found the back of the net once more, half way through the second period, which would finish in being the final score. Nobody predicted a victory in the first game of Hull City's Premier League campaign.

Another highlight of the season happened at the Emirates stadium, Arsenal. After tickets to the fixture had sold out within hours, I had to reluctantly watch the action on the television. The contest had reached half time without a single goal, even though this was Arsenal, one of the big four of English football, a strange positive vibe had swept around the Hull City fans and also players. This feeling appeared to be shot down in a flurry. Within 10 minutes of the second half, Arsenal scored a goal; it was an unfortunate own goal, but still a goal at that. Not to worry, going behind at the Emirates was a very likely outcome for a vast majority of the teams that visit. The next objective in the game now was to make sure we didn't go behind further, just to keep the score-line respectable and maybe this time the pundits wouldn't give us such a hard time, reassuring everybody we would be straight back down into the Championship come May.

What happened next surprised everybody once again. Hull City equalised, a contender for goal of the season had brought the Yorkshire outfit back level in the game with Arsenal. Forget keeping the score line respectable, it looked back on the cards that we could get something from this game. That we did, just four minutes after drawing level with Arsenal, Hull City remarkably took the lead. The score line said 2-1 to Hull City, but nobody was dreaming. This would end up arguably the greatest away victory in Hull's existence.

Fast forward a season and having taken a modest eight points out of a possible 51 in 2009, the morning of the 24th of May looked bleak for Hull City. We had to win and also better the scores from the Newcastle and Middlesbrough games, if we were to stay in the Premier League. It was labelled as the greatest dramatic showdown in recent years, in a bid to stay in the top flight. The task was somehow hardened, as Hull City's opponents on the final day of the campaign were a North West club called Manchester United.

As United were due to play in the final of the Champions League only a few days later and had already won the Premier League title the week before, Sir Alex Ferguson chose to give a great number of the second string team a run out on the hallowed turf of the KC stadium. It was a very tense start for the morning, many people had already feared the worst, it was going to be neigh on impossible to get a result against the champions, even their second string could compete to a high standard in the league and batter most starting elevens. Everybody knew the task was out of our own hands, we had to rely on Aston Villa to get a victory against Newcastle, and hope that Middlesbrough were held to a draw or were defeated in their game.

Although the tension was so high within the stadium, the atmosphere was electric in the capacity crowd. This was nullified half an hour into the game as Manchester United took the lead, through youngster Darron Gibson. Other results at this point were not going in our favour. The tension in the stadium was now increasing by the minute; a quiet airy crowd surrounded the pitch, unsure as to what would happen elsewhere, whether to jump for joy, or wallow in despair.

We all had some sort of communication (but then you wouldn't expect anything else being in the Kingston Communications Stadium), which they used to keep a check on the other results and just before the half time whistle, the most remarkable sight I have ever seen at a football match occurred.
The whole crowd began to cheer in jubilation; a crescendo of noise engulfed the stands within the stadium, as if a goal had been scored. Indeed a goal had been scored, but not at this match, news had travelled through that Aston Villa had taken the lead against Newcastle and it was because of this news, that the cheering had began. It didn't take long for Alan Shearer jokes to start being passed around the mobile phone networks. With all of this happening off the pitch, a majority of the people had forgotten that the main job still wasn't finished.

The second half of the game seemed like an eternity and eventually the final whistle came. Once again the cheering erupted but still the confirmation wasn't solid. A full five more minutes passed before the verification of the result finally came through from Villa Park. Now the party really had started as both Hull City fans and Manchester United fans both began to sing in euphoria as Newcastle United had been relegated out of the Premier League. Phil Brown the Hull manager stole the show as karaoke-style renditions of 'We are staying up' and also 'This is the best trip I have ever been on' were heard first around the Tannoy, but then a choir of around 24,000 people carried on the singsong for minutes afterwards.

After quite a spectacular and often extraordinary season, we live as positive as ever and look to build on what can only be described as an impressive season, fighting against the big teams of the footballing world.

Having been firm favourites to go straight back down and out of the Premier league, Hull City defied the odds and remain a Premier League side for at least one more season.

I'm very happy the season ended as it did and when it did, because I don't think I really could have taken any more of it, well until next year that is!

Thursday 28th May 2009
Song for the day: Ami – No More Worry

Sunderland

It has been four days since the last day of the domestic Premier League campaign and still I am only coming to terms with events that happened that marvellous day.

Today has been the first real day in which my head has finally accepted the events of Sunday, the euphoria of Monday, combined with the 'after the Lord Mayor's show' syndrome of mundane existence since, namely the enormous comedown and the continuation of routine life. To reflect on these events, allowing them their due individual respect, one must look at each individual element and analyse them separately, as to look at them en masse would cause widespread confusion.

- On Sunday it was the final day of the season – Nervy.
- Sunderland were still in danger of going down – Not good.
- More so were Newcastle – Better.
- Boro too were favourites for the drop – Irrelevant.
- One other team – Hull City (the nearest top flight club to the North East by chance)

were the final opponents in this relegation dogfight – Also irrelevant.
- I was at work throughout – Worse still.
- Colleagues were awaiting my footballing doomsday on full show in public – Sickening.
- Hull and the Mags were both losing – Excellent.
- So were we – Bollocks.
- Time had now elapsed into thin air and the clock was ticking down – Irritable.
- The vultures were swarming at work ready for a Newcastle/Hull goal and as a result, my demise – Bastards!
- Sunderland scored – eh?
- Chelsea scored – Predictable.
- Chelsea scored again – Ashley bloody Cole!
- Sunderland scored – Too little too late.
- Final whistle at Hull City 0 United 1 at the KC Stadium– MONUMENTAL!
- Final whistle at Sunderland – Oh well!
- Still no final whistle at Villa Park – Ha'waaaaaayyyy!
- Red card at Villa Park, Newcastle down to 10 men – Nice.
- Full time at Upton Park – Boro are down – Never mind.
- FULL TIME AT VILLA PARK- VILLA 1 NEWCASTLE 0 – ICING ON THE CAKE!
- Within minutes Ricky Sbragia does the decent thing and resigns – The cherry on the top.
- Cue abuse at the TV (aimed at Villa Park) – Told off.
- Go home and celebrate at my mate Eccles' house – Elephant's trunk.
- Our lass has already celebrated too much – Bugger.
- Awoke Monday, got to go to Wembley to watch Burnley and Sheffield United – Mint.
- Arrive at Wembley still celebrating yesterday – Awesome.
- Receive news that I am walking around Wembley's pitch on behalf of the Armed Forces – Amazing.
- Treated like a Rock n' Roll star by both sets of fans in particular – Burnley – Out of this world.
- Free beer and wine – Merry Christmas!
- Congratulate Burnley players on their way up the steps to collect the winning trophy – Memorable.
- More drink – why not?
- The end of the season – Drained and merry.

It is almost Roy of the Rovers stuff, born out of legend…

SHIT YER PANTS SUNDAY

HULL — 0
MAN UTD — 1

VILLA — 1
NEWCASTLE — 0

SUNDERLAND, NEWCASTLE, HULL AND 'BORO' WERE UP FOR THE CHOP.

CHELSEA SCORE AT STADIUM OF LIGHT, 1-0

SUNDERLAND SOMEHOW EQUALISE!

CHELSEA SCORE AGAIN 2-1. WEST HAM ARE BEATING BORO....

— C'MON

...AND I AM SHITTING BRICKS AT WORK!

BORO, HULL AND SUNDERLAND ARE ALL BEATEN BUT THE SUNDERLAND FANS GO WILD AS THE FINAL WHISTLE BLOWS AND NEWCASTLE LOSE TO VILLA! THE MAGS GO DOWN PUTTING THE ICING ON THE CAKE!

← SHEARER

RICKY 'SPAG BOL' RESIGNS.

I FINISH WORK IN TIME FOR TEA AND A CELEBRATORY PISS UP!

sai

Saturday 30th May 2009

Song for the day: UB40 – Signing Off / The Royal Signals TA Band – The Royal Corps of Signals March 'Begone Dull Care'

Sunderland

As I sit down to digest the FA Cup Final between Everton and Chelsea, a big part of me still quivers in shock at the events last weekend. I suppose it will take some time to adjust to the thoughts that Sunderland AFC are the only top flight team in the whole of the North East region. It is not lost on me though how it could have easily turned out different and for the worse.

I console that thought and counteract it with a chuckle at the notion of Newcastle succumbing to the colours of the mighty red and white cloth, as they too will have the pleasure of wearing those colours next season… albeit in the context of a red and white-laden Coca-Cola Championship badge on the sleeves of their playing kit.

Somewhere amongst all the chaos and drama, there was a bloke, often in for ridicule from this particular fan – sometimes over the top emotional anguish, sometimes the harsh truth, which was all the more ghastly. He was asked to do a job for his long term employers, something he probably did not want or need at his time of life, however he stepped into the breech and took the praise and the hits on the chin like a man and like the decent man he was he knew when enough was enough and with supreme dignity, he stepped aside, allowing someone else to have a crack at the arduous role as manager of Sunderland AFC. Ladies and gentlemen, I present to you one Ricky Sbragia. At the end of the day, you somehow kept us up and so respect where respect is due.

If the unforeseen events of the considered big boys of Middlesbrough and Newcastle being relegated to the Championship were refreshing (not because of local rivalries but for the element of surprise) then the season ended in predictable fashion, when Chelsea and Glasgow Rangers lifted their respective cups. More of the same refutable rise of the underdog would be welcome again next season, so long as Sunderland and their yet to be appointed gaffer continue the trend and gatecrash the top half of the table and who knows… maybe European football?

And so as this terrible season draws to an unbelievably dramatic close my bones are aching, my heart rate is calmed and my mind devoid of all logic. Tired and weary with no energy left to carry on, as soon as the transfer window re-opens and the new fixtures are released, I will be invigorated once more, ready to spur the Lads on, batteries recharged, soul illuminated to shine at the Stadium of Light, slate wiped clean, we all begin with a fresh start, fickle as we all are, but then that is the game of football, transfixed in the middle of a North Eastern way of life.

Haaaaaawwwwwwwaaaaaaayyyyyyyy!

DESPAIR

RELIEF

ACCEPTENCE

JUBILATION

| **2008/09** The Post Mortem

How often in one single season does an entire region's football clubs find themselves all scrapping for survival? Add to that the fact that the nearest top flight club to the North East region, Hull City, were also deep in the mire is astounding. It was akin to the football negative equity equivalent of the National Lottery, all our numbers came up at once and then some.

As with the lottery, luck played its part, both good and fortunate for Hull and Sunderland, whilst the final countdown was in motion for the other two unfortunate souls – Middlesbrough and Newcastle. In a post mortem exercise, the norm is to investigate what went wrong, how it happened and lessons to be learnt for future improvement.

If the four shells of football clubs were dissected, come the close of the 2008/09 campaign, one would locate a common denominator of lack of quality, crippled with inconsistency. Two out of the four were lucky to survive, arguing that they have both suffered injustice before and maybe it was time for the Premier League stalwarts to encounter life beyond the big boys. Representatives from the Tyne and the Tees would argue this would be a case of sour grapes.

One thing is for sure though - amongst all of the bickering on the rights and wrongs, the refereeing decisions and the luck of the brave and who's football club is bigger than the other, football's once notorious hotbed stood still for one moment and in that time, the rest of the game kicked on elsewhere, bypassing the region, leaving it to lurk in the shadows of forgotten glories.

Now we must dust ourselves down, eat a slice of humble pie, take a long good hard look at ourselves and start over again. It is what our forefathers did in hard times in past generations and something we all must look to do now, lifting our football clubs, our lifeblood, away from the uncertain perils of administration and bottom half of the table finishes, aiming for the stars. It is after all, no less than what these good people deserve.

| **Glossary** Of Terms and Abbreviations

SOL – An abbreviation of Sunderland AFC's home ground – The Sunderland Stadium of Light.

Mackems – Nickname for someone hailing from Sunderland and Wearside. Considered by some to be derogatory, others think of it as a source of identity.

Castle Grey Skull – Mimicking name for the home of Newcastle United – St. James' Park.

Sid James' – Another form of negative banter towards St. James'.

Smoggies – Nickname term for someone residing from Middlesbrough and the residing areas, due to the Chemical works and heavy industrial area around the town.

Manky – North East slang for the word dirty.

Heed – Nickname and abbreviation for local non-league side Gateshead.

Baysiders – Nickname of local non-league side Whitley Bay.

Baggies – Nickname for 2008/09 Premier League side West Bromwich Albion.

Ricky Spag Bol – Fans' affectionate nickname for Sunderland manager Ricky Sbragia, as this was easier to pronounce than his surname. Half Scot, half Italian, the nickname kept in tradition with his roots.

FMTTM – Abbreviation for Middlesbrough fanzine Fly Me To The Moon.

Marley Potts – A suburb of the City of Sunderland.

Yarm – Affluent suburb of Cleveland.

Stockton – Nearby local town, residing on the River Tees, adjacent to Middlesbrough.

Darlo – Local abbreviation for the town of Darlington.

Dunston Rocket – A set of high-rise flats in Dunston, Gateshead, which have seen better days.

Spuggy – Character from Tyneside kids' show in the early 90s, Byker Grove.

Smack My Bitch Up Video – Reference to The Prodigy's No. 1 hit record video, in which a range of shenanigans are shown, from excessive drinking to lesbian brawls and so a referral to this means one had a bloody good night out!

Penshaw Monument – A monument found overlooking Sunderland, which is also incorporated into the SAFC club badge.

BFBS - Abbreviation of British Forces Broadcasting Service. Does what it says on the tin.

'Managerial fishes' – Author's own term referring to the film The Godfather in which the character Luca Brasi is killed by the mob and the way his friends are told of his death is by sending a fish in the post. This itself refers to an old Sicilian saying 'sleeping with the fishes' meaning he has been killed. In this sense, the Sunderland manager was on borrowed time.

Gentleman's Bar – Not of the lap-dancing variety of crotch-less knickers ilk, but rather the name for the gentlemen only bar in the Mill View Social Club in Fulwell, Sunderland. A rare piece of old tradition still enacting in this modern age.

MackemEnemy – The derogatory term used for ex- Sunderland manager Lawrie McMenemy. After being blamed for the torrid relegation of the club to the third tier of English football, the fans changed his name accordingly.

BBC Football Predictor – The computerised form of predicting the football tables, when inserting scores of your choice. A clever piece of kit, which can play havoc with one's mind come the end of season permutations.

'tezzas' – Slang, abbreviation for a man's testicles, balls, gonads, knackers etc.

Jacky White's Market – An indoor market in Sunderland city centre.

Gooners – Nickname term for an Arsenal supporter.

Barcodes – Derogatory label for a Newcastle fan, linking the black and white colours to a barcode.

Toon – Nickname for Newcastle, changing town to Geordie speak – Toon.

Hand of God – Incident in the 1986 Mexico World Cup, where a dirty little Argie decided to cheat his way to the World Cup Semi-Finals by using his hand instead of his head, knocking England out at the same time, which has caused no bitterness since, honest!

SJP – Abbreviation for St. James' Park, Newcastle.

Merc – Abbreviation for a Mercedes Benz automobile.

A19 – Stretch of Dual Carriageway linking Newcastle, Sunderland and Middlesbrough.

Skunks – Derogatory term for Newcastle, once again linking the clubs' colours with the wild animal.

Teesborough League – Local non-league format based in and around Middlesbrough.

Hurworth – Home of Middlesbrough FC's training ground in Rockcliffe Park, Hurworth.

Haaaaaaaawwwwwaaaaaaaaayyyyyyyy! – Excitable scream from a typical North East football fan. Spelt differently in local dialects, it is 'Howay' for Tyneside and Northumberland and 'Ha'way' for Wearside and beyond. Do not get the two mixed up!

| **Bibliography** Newspapers, magazines and other media

A Love Supreme

BBC Look North

BBC Radio Tees

BFBS Radio

Come On Boro

The Evening Gazette

The Evening Chronicle

Fly Me To The Moon

Four Four Two

The Guardian

The Journal

The Irish Times

The Northern Echo

Players Inc

Ready To Go

Radio Newcastle

Sky Sports News

The Sun

The Sunderland Echo

When Saturday Comes

Wikipedia

| **Biographies** of Authors

Robert Nichols is the editor of Fly Me To The Moon Middlesbrough fanzine and editor of the website fmttm.com He has contributed in editing two Boro fanzine annuals and he was also a partner in the Teesside Urban Legends – A Best of the 'Boro Message Boards. Accompanying his writing experience, Robert has also released a couple of football songs including The Tony Mowbray Testimonial Single. He has featured heavily on radio and television, including BBC's Look North programme. Robert has been a music columnist in the Middlesbrough Gazette for nearly 15 years.

Barry Hindmarch is a regular columnist for Players Inc North East football magazine and is an ardent Newcastle United supporter. He has contributed on the book publication – Wor Al – a tribute to United legend – Alan Shearer. Away from football, Barry has also written various military articles for Durham Town & Country magazine, as well as appearing in the Newcastle Evening Chronicle on a regular basis.

Malcolm Robinson works at RAF Lyneham in Wiltshire as a Movements Controller. Since joining up in 2003, he has served the Royal Air Force around the globe, including Cyprus, Jordan, Canada, Iraq and Afghanistan. Outside of work, Malcolm is an avid freelance writer and photographer and he has been a writer for A Love Supreme Magazine for over 10 years. He also writes for Players Inc Magazine and various other publications. In 2007, Malcolm published his first book – From Afghanistan To Temazepam, after featuring in a collection of football short stories the previous year in the book – 24 Hour SAFC People. He has featured significantly in the media, especially in the current football season, appearing on the front page of the Sunderland Echo twice, featured in The Sun, was the subject of a Talk Sport Radio phone-in, alongside several magazine articles on a recent mission to see Sunderland play in Jersey. He is the new assistant editor of www.safcpride.com